# FOURTEEN

## to there and back

*A J Bazz*

Published by New Generation Publishing in 2024

Copyright © A J Bazz 2024

First Edition

The author asserts the moral right under the Copyright, Designs and Patents Act 1988 to be identified as the author of this work.

All Rights reserved. No part of this publication may be reproduced, stored in a retrieval system or transmitted, in any form or by any means without the prior consent of the author, nor be otherwise circulated in any form of binding or cover other than that which it is published and without a similar condition being imposed on the subsequent purchaser.

Paperback ISBN: 9781835633298
Hardback ISBN: 9781835633304

www.newgeneration-publishing.com

New Generation Publishing

# Contents

PROLOGUE ................................................................. 1
THE EARLY YEARS .................................................... 2
CHAPTER 1 THE DOODLEBUG ................................. 3
CHAPTER 2 BOYS WILL BE BOYS! ........................... 5
CHAPTER 3 PLAYING TRUANT ............................... 10
CHAPTER 4 EVACUATION ....................................... 14
CHAPTER 5 SATURDAY PICTURES ........................ 18
CHAPTER 6 FIRST JOB ............................................. 24
CHAPTER 7 NEW HOUSE ......................................... 28
CHAPTER 8 FIRST BUSINESS ................................. 33
TO WORK .................................................................. 40
CHAPTER 9 APPRENTICESHIP ............................... 41
CHAPTER 10 THE CLUB ........................................... 46
CHAPTER 11 OUTINGS ............................................ 55
CHAPTER 12 AUSTRIA ............................................. 61
CHAPTER 13 LIFE AND DEATH .............................. 66
GROWING UP ........................................................... 71
CHAPTER 14 NATIONAL SERVICE ......................... 72
CHAPTER 15 MOVING ON ....................................... 79
CHAPTER 16 BORED ................................................ 91
CHAPTER 17 CAPTURED ......................................... 98
CIVVY STREET ....................................................... 105
CHAPTER 18 CIVVY STREET ................................ 106
CHAPTER 19 A NEW BEGINNING ........................ 115

| Chapter | Title | Page |
|---|---|---|
| CHAPTER 20 | STAFF PROBLEMS | 119 |
| CHAPTER 21 | BANK OF ENGLAND | 122 |
| CHAPTER 22 | NEW HOME, NEW PROBLEMS | 124 |
| CHAPTER 23 | CHANGES | 130 |
| CHAPTER 24 | AGENT ABROAD | 136 |
| CHAPTER 25 | BETAN | 144 |
| CHAPTER 26 | TRY AGAIN | 149 |
| CHAPTER 27 | IN THE LIMELIGHT | 155 |
| CHAPTER 28 | WELCOME WAGON | 161 |
| CHAPTER 29 | NEW OFFICE AND NEW CONVENTIONS | 167 |
| CHAPTER 30 | QE2 | 182 |
| CHAPTER 31 | ANOTHER BUSINESS | 186 |
| CHAPTER 32 | MR ROCHESTER | 191 |
| CHAPTER 33 | THE WRIT | 198 |
| CHAPTER 34 | BROKEN FUN | 203 |
| CHAPTER 35 | PICKWICK CLUB | 209 |
| CHAPTER 36 | SEMINARS | 215 |
| CHAPTER 37 | THE DEMON DRINK | 223 |
| CHAPTER 38 | CZECHOSLOVAKIA | 229 |
| CHAPTER 39 | FIFTY | 235 |
| CHAPTER 40 | CLUB, SEMINAR AND WEDDING | 239 |
| CHAPTER 41 | QE2 SEMINAR | 242 |
| CHAPTER 42 | THE WEDDING | 244 |
| CHAPTER 43 | NEW TRADE | 247 |
| CHAPTER 44 | ARCHITECTS | 252 |
| EPILOGUE | | 259 |

# Author's Note

The true story of a poorly educated, mildly dyslexic lad born before the Second World War and his journey through life who always believed he would one day be a millionaire.

The events and incidents actually happened; however, some characters' names have been changed. With the passing of time, the actual words spoken in conversation may not be strictly accurate.

# Acknowledgements

I would like to thank Paula for her help and hours of work she has put in to prepare this book, Joan for the thirty turbulent years working together, and my wife Mavis for her support and putting up with me. She is sadly no longer with us. She always wanted me to have a steady job; sorry, dear, I would have been bored to tears.

# Dedication

For my granddaughters Charlotte, Alice, and Millie.
Now you know what Grandpa was doing during his life
until the year 2000.

# Prologue

An almighty scream rang out down the corridor, so loud and piercing that it hurt the ears. It seemed to be coming from a darkened ward. The Sister, dressed in her immaculate blue uniform with white cuffs and collar ran down the corridor towards the sound. Pushing open the door, she was greeted by two nurses trying to assist the lady in the bed.

"What's going in here?" she said to the nearest nurse.

"She's in labour, Sister."

"I can see that, but why the screaming?"

"It was me," said the other nurse. "Look at the baby's face and head, it's horrible."

Sister looked down as the baby was at last coming into the world. Its face flat and squashed with its nose flat against the rest of its face, it was all red with little ears pinched to the side of its head, looking like some mini monster.

Having taken one quick look, the Sister broke the skin around the neck and took the membrane off its little head. "It's a caul," she said. "You have to take it off quickly so that the baby can breathe. It's very rare, possibly only one in a million, and very lucky. Sailors try to get their hands on the caul; they say that they will never drown if they have one."

The baby let out a loud howl. "He will have a loud voice," said the Sister. "You have a little boy, Mrs Walker. What are you going to call him?"

"Barry," she said.

It was June 1937.

# THE EARLY YEARS

# Prologue

An almighty scream rang out down the corridor, so loud and piercing that it hurt the ears. It seemed to be coming from a darkened ward. The Sister, dressed in her immaculate blue uniform with white cuffs and collar ran down the corridor towards the sound. Pushing open the door, she was greeted by two nurses trying to assist the lady in the bed.

"What's going in here?" she said to the nearest nurse.

"She's in labour, Sister."

"I can see that, but why the screaming?"

"It was me," said the other nurse. "Look at the baby's face and head, it's horrible."

Sister looked down as the baby was at last coming into the world. Its face flat and squashed with its nose flat against the rest of its face, it was all red with little ears pinched to the side of its head, looking like some mini monster.

Having taken one quick look, the Sister broke the skin around the neck and took the membrane off its little head. "It's a caul," she said. "You have to take it off quickly so that the baby can breathe. It's very rare, possibly only one in a million, and very lucky. Sailors try to get their hands on the caul; they say that they will never drown if they have one."

The baby let out a loud howl. "He will have a loud voice," said the Sister. "You have a little boy, Mrs Walker. What are you going to call him?"

"Barry," she said.

It was June 1937.

# THE EARLY YEARS

# Chapter 1

## The Doodlebug

"Dot, Dot come quickly, it's a doodle bug!" came the cry from Mrs Longton who lived next door.

"Where?" said Dot looking up to the sky.

"Listen," said Mrs Longton. The sound was like a big tin full of loose nuts and bolts rattling around or a giant's football rattle being played in time.

"Look, there it is!" said Barry, who had just come out the back door, pointing to the flying machine.

The doodlebug looked like a big cigar with two small stubby wings, but was, in fact, a German rocket called a V1.

"Cor, look at the flames coming out the back; they are all red and yellow, a bit like a dragon."

"Christ, I hope those flames don't stop."

"Why, what happens then?"

"As soon as the engine stops the flames stop coming out and it dives straight down," said Mum pointing her flat hand at the ground.

By now the neighbours were all coming out of their houses and looking up. All were women in their pinafores, some wiping their hands on old cloths. They were looking worried wondering when the engine would stop, silently praying.

"Mum, I think it's going to hit those houses at the end of our garden," said Barry.

"Oh my god!"

The noise suddenly stopped, a cry went up, *"NO!"* The flames ceased and the doodlebug turned nose down for the ground making an ear-splitting sound. Some of the women screamed.

God was with them. The rocket missed the houses by no more than the length of a football pitch and flew over the road and with an almighty bang, flames flying in the air, it crashed into the chalk pit.

The houses were set around a hollow green with a small road running around three quarters of the green for the use of fire engines, coal deliveries and the milkman. Small paths led up the banks to the path in front of the houses. The houses were of red brick, semi-detached with sloping red roofs each side; they were modern in the 1930s but did not have bathrooms. They had the luxury of an inside toilet, a coal-fired boiler in one corner of the kitchen made of brick with a metal pot for heating the water for washing clothes. The hot water was also used to fill a tin bath which was taken down from the wall on Friday nights for the family bath.

In another downstairs room was a black coal-fired cast iron stove which was cleaned with black polish every week; fire was kept in day and night, with a kettle boiling most of the time to make tea. On the front of the stove an iron door would open into the oven.

At the back of the houses a long garden was planted with vegetables except for the air raid shelter which looked like a grass bank. The shelter was partly under the ground and made of corrugated tin covered in earth with grass laid on top. Inside were four bunk beds, no heating or electric light and just a bucket for a toilet.

In the event of an air raid, the siren, which was on a long pole behind the nearby fire station, would let out a long warning sound and everyone in the area would go down into the shelters.

# Chapter 2

# Boys will be Boys!

Barry and Carol were playing on the green in front of the houses, both about six years old, the war had not yet ended. It was a lovely warm sunny day, and they were playing doctors and nurses.

"Let's go into that dip by the path, it can be your bed in the hospital," said Barry.

"OK," said Carol. They both moved into the dip and lay down.

"Shall I show you my bits?"

"Why?"

"Well, they are different from boys."

"Why are they different?" said Barry looking interested.

"I don't know but I've seen my brother's willy, it's like a worm. But mine's different, look," said Carol pulling down her knickers, pulling up her dress and opening her legs. Barry bent his head down to have a good look.

"Can I touch it?" said Barry.

"If you like." Barry was just about to put his finger out to touch when suddenly he heard a loud scraping noise.

"Barry Walker, I can see you, stop that!" said a very loud voice. It was Mrs Longton looking out of her upstairs window.

Carol pulled her knickers up very quickly wobbling her little bum, pulled down her dress and ran across the green to her house. Barry ran home wondering if Mrs Longton would tell Mum.

The bombing was now getting very bad, and Barry's little brother was only a few months old. His Mum said to him one day, "Barry, we are going away for a little while."

"Does that mean I don't have to go to school?"
"You will have to go to a new school."
"I don't want to go then!"

Barry and his mates liked to play down the chalk pits which were nearby. They would cross the green up the lane and cross over the main road to the lane that led down to the railway near to the River Thames. Girls were not allowed to come with them as they could not be cowboys or Tarzan, nor climb trees. The boys liked to play in the jungle which was near the sewage works.

"Look," said Brian as he sat on the top of the level crossing gate pointing towards the river, "I wonder where that ship's going; do you think it's going to India?"

"No," said Barry, "there's still a war on out there."

"Perhaps it will get dived on by the jerry planes."

"Don't be daft, they got no planes left," said Barry as he put both arms out to his sides. "Arrrr, arrrr, arrrr!" he shouted. "Look out, I'm a Spitfire," as he dived down onto Brian.

The boys went into the woods – which they called the jungle – and started to swing from the trees and the vines that grew on them. "I'm hungry," said Barry, "let's find some liquorice wood." After some time they found the wood, which was about one to two inches thick, like a vine with a lined grey bark and black wood inside. They pulled the bark off and started to suck as they walked towards the edge of the jungle.

"Look, there's the sewage works and the allotments. Let's see if there's something to eat," said Barry.

Barry and Brian walked on the grass paths between the allotments where they could see lots of vegetables growing. Barry pulled up two carrots, giving one to Brian.

"But it's got dirt on it," said Brian.

"Wipe it on your jumper if you are that fussy," said Barry putting his carrot into his mouth and chewing it, dirt and all. "Here look, tomatoes," he said through a mouthful

# Chapter 6

# First Job

Walking home from school, he could see an older boy just in front of him walking down the hill towards the green in front of the houses where they both lived. Barry walked faster and caught up with him. "Hello, Jim, what's Father Christmas going to bring you?"

"There isn't any Father Christmas."

"Yes, there is!" said Barry looking at Jim with a frown on his face.

"No there isn't."

"Then who brings all the presents?" Barry started to cry. With tears glistening on the edge of his eyes and his cheeks turning red, he started to get upset as he looked up at Jim.

"Don't be daft; it's your Mum and Dad that put them there."

"No, they don't," said Barry, as he ran away crying.

From that day on, Barry knew there was no such person as Father Christmas, but he did not realise there were to be many more illusions shattered during his lifetime.

As the year wore on and with winter fast approaching, the weather started to get cold. Barry decided to get a job because he wanted some money to buy sweets. He did not have pocket money as his parents could not afford it; all their money was spent on rent, fuel and food. Coal was going up in price and food and many other items were still rationed.

On Saturday, Nick the milkman, called to collect the milk money as he did every week. Barry's Mum went into the other room to get the money from one of the tins. She

"Are you alright?"

"Yes, I'll be alright," thinking what he was going to tell Mum! He got up, his clothes still dripping.

"Are you sure?"

"Yes."

"Well, you be careful now," said the man as he walked off the barge.

*She will kill me*, thought Barry, *I'd better take my clothes off and try to dry them*. Barry started to take his clothes off and began to ring them out, screwing them with his hands. More wet patches showing on the deck.

He stood there with no clothes on and laid out his vest, short trousers, socks and shirt in the sun. Luckily for him it was a warm day and he lay down in the sun to dry himself off. He started to doze, dreaming about his adventures around the world. He awoke! How long had he been asleep? What time was it? *Crumbs, I'd better get home!*

Once dressed, he started to make his way home, having been out all day with only a plain bread roll to eat. As he neared home, he wondered what his Mum would say.

"Where have you been?" his Mum shouted, glaring at him with tears in her eyes. She gave a sigh of relief, her worrying was over. "Have you eaten?"

"No, Mum."

"Sit down, boy, I'll get you some bread and dripping."

all the countries around the world. The colours, the smells, people of different races and languages.

Deep in thought, he soon found himself down by the river where the tide was up. Looking around as he walked along the grass bank, he could see a timber walkway jutting out into the river with barges at the end. *Great, more things to explore!* he thought as he almost ran along the jetty towards the barges.

He jumped on board the nearest one and nearly lost his footing. His left leg dangling over the side, he made a grab for the side of the container hole where they fill the barges. The sides were raised to keep the cargo from spilling over the sides and into the river. Once on board he started to explore, walking around the deck, looking out across the river shouting, "AHOY THERE!" to the tugs going up and down the river. Moving around the deck he suddenly slipped on a wet patch. SPLASH! Into the water he went, down into the murky darkness.

Suddenly, he rose to the surface, his face contorted and dripping water, splashing around with his arms and shouting, "I CAN'T SWIM!"

Still shouting, Barry suddenly noticed a man on the river bank running towards him. He kept moving his arms in a circular motion which just kept him afloat. The man climbed on to the barge with a long pole. "Grab hold of the pole, quickly, son." Barry splashed his way towards the pole and made a grab for it with one hand, but his hand began to slip. He was moving towards the barge. He grabbed with his other hand and now holding with two hands, the man pulled him on board. Barry lay on the deck trying to get his breath, looking like a drowning rat, water dripping off his clothes and running out of his short trousers and down his legs. He shivered a bit in the warm sunshine.

"Thanks, Mister," he cried, spitting out salty water.

"How did you fall in?"

"I slipped."

judging by their sacking bags, had been shopping in Gravesend.

The little boy had just asked his Mum if he could have a sweet. His sister, skipping alongside, said "Can I have one, Mum?"

Their mother was flustered and struggling to carry the bags. "You can both have a sweet when we get on board the ferry, now behave."

Barry got on board and started to explore. He looked around the decks and watched the wash from the propeller, all frothy and white in the grey water just like soap suds in his bath water on a Friday evening. He looked around, across the river, watching the tugs pulling barges. Some had four, one was towing six and he wondered what was in them. Up river, he could see a ship coming down, heading for the sea, smoke belching from the funnel. *I wonder where it's going*, he thought.

He made his way up to the top deck so he could get a better view as the crew cast off. The ferry by now had many passengers with children. Barry put his hand up over his eyes to keep the sun out as he looked back at Gravesend, pretending he was a captain of a ship on the high seas going to some exotic country.

The ferry soon docked on the Tilbury side of the river with the passengers pushing to get off. Barry looked down the stairway, watching, and he turned around and ran up the stairs to the top deck. The ferry was filling up with people wanting to go to Gravesend and soon it left the pier. Barry spent some hours going back and forth between Gravesend and Tilbury, playing captain of a ship travelling the high seas.

Walking off the ferry and up the hill to the end of Gravesend High Street, Barry suddenly remembered he had no money left for his fare home. *Well, I will have to walk home*, he thought to himself and started to walk towards Northfleet. As he walked, he was thinking of the sea and all the exciting adventures he would have visiting stage whose birthday it is today. Whose birthday is it?" Six hands went up with the kids shouting 'MINE'. The manager, pointing to one of the usherettes, said, "The little girl with the pigtails, who pushed her way through the other children to the side." She was in a pink and white dress, a hand-me-down from her big sister and very worn. On her feet were light grey socks which had seen better days as white.

Holding the hand of the usherette, she skipped as she was led to the stage. She stood with the other kids in a line on the stage waiting her turn to be given a small bag containing two sweets, an apple, and a little book. "What is your name?"

"It's Dolly," said the little girl, "and I'm six and a half."

The film finished and the kids started to leave the theatre still making a noise, calling names, pushing and pulling. Barry hung back waiting until the mass of bodies had gone through to the exit. There was lots of time before he had to catch his bus home; he thought, *What shall I do?* Once outside, he looked across the road, across to the chimney stacks of the factories in the pits on the other side of the road, some of which were belching dirty white smoke. He could see the river behind with the ships going down to the sea. He put his hand in his pocket and felt the penny which was just enough for his bus fare home. He looked again across to the water and turned right towards Gravesend, away from his bus stop.

Making his way down the hill through the streets to the pier where the Tilbury ferry docked, he wondered if a penny was enough for the fare. He passed buildings where large timber poles were helping to hold up walls next to piles of rubbish and bricks where a house used to be. The war damage was slowly being repaired. Arriving at the ferry booth, Barry paid his fare of one penny and walked down the covered-in gang plank following a family who,

As the bus continued, he noticed the remains of some houses which had been hit by German bombs or doodlebugs and which were close to some of the cement works which had also been hit. As the bus started to go up the hill into Northfleet, Barry descended the stairs ready to jump off.

"Oi, watch it," the bus conductor shouted to Barry as he jumped off the bus which was still moving.

Barry crossed the road and followed the lovely smell of newly baked bread to the small shop to buy his warm bread roll for a ha'penny. He walked on to the flea pit, the local name for the cinema, possibly because the kids were always coming home scratching their heads with fleas or nits. Eating his roll, he was deep in thought thinking about the pictures, *Tom Mix and Roy Rogers* and if he should go up on the stage and pretend it was his birthday to get a present.

The kids were all queuing to get in, chattering, the boys trying to pull the girls pigtails, calling each other names and making a hell of noise. One little girl was crying. "He pulled my hair," she sobbed to the bigger girl next to her.

"Oh, shut up, Alice. Just bash him one, he'll soon stop."

Finally, the doors opened, and all the kids went in nearly knocking over the man opening the doors; the noise of the kids shouting, the pushing, the girls screaming, and his face screwed up in pain!

The black and white films started with a Cowboy and Indian staring Roy Rogers. It was just getting to the Indians chasing the Cowboys when the film broke down making a screeching noise and the screen jumped up and down. The kids went wild, jumping on their seats and shouting. The lights came up and the manager came on to the stage. "Girls and boys," he shouted, trying to make himself heard. He tried again louder. "Girls and boys!" he shouted above the noise. "While we are waiting for the film to start again, we shall have the children up on the

# Chapter 5

# Saturday Pictures

"Mum, can I go to pictures on Saturday?"

"We will see."

"Thanks, Mum," said Barry, knowing that "We will see" was a yes!

Saturday came and Mum gave Barry sixpence. "Here you are," she said, giving him the money from her purse. "That will pay for your bus fare, the pictures, and a bread roll."

"Thanks, Mum."

Barry almost ran out of the house, down the path and through the avenue which was lined each side of the road with tall trees. The sun was just starting to filter through throwing shadows across the road which Barry tried to jump over as he made his way to the main road to catch the bus to Northfleet.

It was a lovely sunny day as he boarded the bus and Barry paid the conductor his half penny for the fare and ran up the stairs to sit on the top deck so that he could see across to the River Thames. The road was undulating, some small hills and some steep, and as the bus reached the top of the hills Barry could see on the right the woods which he and his mates called the jungle where they sometimes played. The trees, bushes and brambles had grown up when the chalk was finished, and the pits were left by the cement companies.

On the left-hand side he could see the ships going up and down the river, some belching out dirty smoke. Barry dreamed of going to sea and seeing the world; he thought of the map that hung on the wall at school with most of the countries coloured pink being part of the British Empire.

"Mum, have I got to go to school?"

"Yes, you have."

"But I don't know anyone."

"You will soon make friends."

Barry sulked away into the playground. Looking around for some boys to talk to, he went up to them, standing near and watching. "Can I play?" he said.

The boys stopped playing and looked at him. "Don't 'e talk funny?" said a small ruddy-faced boy with light hair.

The boys all came close around Barry. "Where do you come from?" they said looking at him, some pulling funny faces. One boy pointed his finger, stabbing Barry in his belly and began to push him.

The teacher who was standing near the school building gave a shout, "Stop that, Tommy, or I'll send you to the Head." At that moment the bell rang, and they all began to file into the school.

Barry had been given sandwiches for his lunch, but he did not want to eat in school with the other boys and girls. At lunchtime, he went down to the town and stood under an arch to eat his sandwiches feeling very miserable.

sure you would like to make them up yourself, Mrs Walker."

The room was big with two beds and a cot for little Richard, a wardrobe and a set of drawers. The floor was the same colour as the panels in the hall with two brown and cream mats. Barry's Mum started to unpack while Barry jumped on one of the beds to look out of the window.

"Mum, look at the garden, there are lots of paths and some have got wooden poles with roses growing up them and look, there's a stream at the bottom. Can we go and look?"

"After we have been down for tea." Having got little Richard ready, they went downstairs to tea.

Mrs Johnson met them at the bottom of the stairs. "Have you all settled in? Do you like your room? Come into the drawing room," said Mrs Johnson, not waiting for an answer.

"Mum, what's a drawing room?" whispered Barry.

Mum pulled a funny face, "Shush."

They looked around as they followed her into the drawing room, which had the same wood panels as the hall.

"Come and sit down, and let's have some tea."

Barry's eyes nearly popped out of his head. There in front of him on the table, which was covered in a bright white cloth, stood a tall cake stand. Barry had never seen one before; it was full of different kinds of cakes. Butter scones, fruit scones, fruit cake slices and even two cream cakes!

Mrs Johnson picked up the silver tea pot, "How would you like your tea, dear, white with sugar?"

The next day was Barry's first day at school. He held on to his packed lunch in a brown paper bag and watched the kids, who were running and jumping, all enjoying themselves.

ticket collectors and other officials checked their labels and put them on the right trains. Barry thought it was great fun being on a steam train. He tried to look out the open window, but Mum tried to pull him back. "You'll get dirt in your eyes, come back in," she said trying to hold the baby with one hand and pull at his short trousers with the other.

They arrived at Bovey Tracey feeling worn out and tired, to be met by an old, official looking lady. "Mrs Walker?" said the sour-faced lady, looking and sounding as though she had just eaten a lemon. "Come with me," she said as she marched off, striding up the hill.

Barry, carrying the bag, Mum carrying Richard and her case and trying to keep up, they came to a big, detached house, three storeys high surrounded by roses. His Mum's face dropped in amazement and Barry said, "Cor." They passed through a rose arch and the sour-faced lady knocked at the door.

The lady who answered the door was very smart in her floral frock with blue and pink flowers. Barry thought she was not like old sour face. She smiled. "Hello, do come in. You must be Mrs Walker, and your children. Let me show you to your room and when you have settled in, you must come down and have some tea in the front parlour," she said.

Having carefully wiped their shoes on the mat, they followed the lady up the stairs. Looking around, Barry noticed a grandfather clock in the hall; even his little brother turned his head as the clock ticked. The walls in the hallway were panelled in dark wood, but as they ascended the stairs light filtered in from a window, casting beams of sunlight, specks of dust glinting like fairy lights in the beams.

They followed the nice lady up two flights of stairs, where she opened a door to a big room under the roof. "I have asked Anne to make up your beds for tonight, but I'm

# Chapter 4

## Evacuation

Art, Barry's father, worked in an aircraft factory in Ashford, Middlesex, and had to leave home at 5 o'clock each morning to catch a train to London and then another train to Ashford. One day, after Art had gone to work, Barry's Mum sat him down and said, "We are going away for a little while."

Barry was full questions.

"Is Dad coming?"

"No, he has to work."

"Is Richard coming with us?"

"Yes, he's only a baby and you have to help me look after him."

"Where are we going, Mum? Have I got to go to school?"

"We are going on a train to Bovey Tracey in Devon, and you will have to go to school."

"Where's that?"

"It's a long way away, but there will be other boys on the train, and you will make new friends at school."

A few days later Barry, his little baby brother, and Mum were standing in a line at the railway station. Mum had an old brown case containing their clothes, a cloth bag with nappies and sandwiches for the journey. Mum had on her best coat and hat with a feather sticking out the top. All had their gas masks in small, light brown boxes tied up with string and hanging around their necks. The station was crowded with children – some with their mothers, older ones on their own – and all had labels around their necks. Little ones crying, older children shouting and playing games, they filed through to catch their trains. The

who was still waving the stick and hitching up her dress and pinafore to get over the fence. "I'll get you, you little sod, you wait until I get you home."

Hearing the noise, the other ladies moved down to their gates as Barry came running by. He was beginning to puff, his breathing in short gasps, his face going red.

One lady was shouting, "Go on, Dot, get him, give him a beating!"

They all joined in. "Go on, Dot, catch him, catch the little bugger, give him a whack."

A lady began to open her gate to try and catch Barry, but he was too quick dodging around her. He ran like the wind as though his very life depended on it and ran indoors, nearly falling over as he went up the stairs into his room slamming the door. His back to the door, his chest heaving and almost crying, waiting for his Mum to come in.

His Mum did not go up the stairs; she was still trying to catch her breath, thinking what to do about Barry as she started to put the washing in the boiler.

Some hours later Barry crept down the stairs and into the kitchen. "I'm sorry, Mum," he said almost crying. "I'm hungry; can I have something to eat?"

His Mum melted, she could no longer be angry. "Don't you ever play truant again," she said as she went to get the bread out to make Barry a slice of dripping bread with salt.

Barry did play truant again, being led by what must have been the leader of the four boys. They went into the wood yard near the hoardings, running and climbing on the wood and being chased off by Bill the local Policeman. One of the boys was caught and received a slap around the ear from Bill. "If I catch you boys in this yard again, I shall take you to the station and get your Mums to come and collect you."

The boys did not go into the wood yard again; they were too frightened of Bill and what he would do.

Brian turned to the boys. "When she starts to talk to old Wellington boots, go through the gate and hide behind the wall. We can then go to the pit without him seeing us."

The pit was a mile away at the side of the main road on the way back to Barry's home. They managed to get out of the playground, a rag bag of four boys in scruffy short trousers, some with patches stitched over holes, others with dirty marks where they had sat down in the dirt. Their socks all down around their ankles, shoes all with scuff marks from kicking stones and playing football.

Having run, played and chased their way to the hoardings just above the pit, they climbed over the low wire and hid behind the advertising hoardings to make a camp. The hoardings were in the shape of a 'V' lying on its side with the bottom of the 'V' facing across the road pointing towards the road leading to the fire station. All along one side were terraced houses with fences dividing the short gardens which led up to the front doors.

Outside most of the houses ladies were talking as they leaned across the fence. All were wearing pinafores, some of which looked coloured and one or two were made from sack cloth. A number of them had curlers in their hair with a cloth partly draped over them; old slippers with toes sticking out, thick brown stockings rolled down to their ankles, talking about the war and hoping their husbands were safe, how to find food for the kids and many other subjects affecting their daily lives.

The boys took it in turns to try out smoking the fag, passing it from one to another, puffing away. "I feel funny," said one boy turning a little green. Suddenly, all hell let loose, and a face appeared looking around the hoarding.

"Barry Walker, what are you doing? Why aren't you at school, you little bugger? Come out of there," said Mrs Walker waving a stick. "And you lot go home!"

Barry got up very quickly and ran around the side and over the fence on to the road, followed by Mrs Walker,

# Chapter 3

# Playing Truant

The boys were bored and fed up with school; there were four of them in the same class, Brian, Richard, Mick, and Barry. They had been chatting in the playground. "Let's go," said one of the boys.

"Go where?" said two of the others, Brian and Richard.

"I know, we could go and play down by the chalk pit," commented Barry. "You know, behind those big boards."

"I got a fag; we could all have a drag," said Mick.

"OK, let's go," said Barry.

"But what about old Wellington boots, he's standing over there," said Richard, pointing to the door into the school. "If he sees us, we'll get the cane and I don't want that again," he said rubbing his bum, "it hurt."

"I got an idea. Rose, come here," said Barry.

"What for?" said Rose.

"I'll give you a sweet," said Barry.

Rose came skipping over. She was a small girl for her age, thin with a dirty dress, which had

been her older sister's handed down and was far too large, looking like it had been made from

cheap old curtains.

Barry said, "I'll give you this sweet if you go and talk to Mr Wellington."

"What about?" said Rose.

"I don't know; tell him you have wet your knickers. No, tell him they are falling down and has he got a pin," said Barry.

"Give me the sweet then," said Rose.

"No, you can't take them out, they're the ones growing wild; did you know those seeds have been through hundreds of people?"

"You mean they have eaten them and then poo'd them out?" said Barry.

"I feel sick," said Brian, turning a funny colour and holding his belly.

Barry had just gone seven and his little brother was just over one year old; Barry was looking forward to Father Christmas coming to bring him and his brother presents. It was late 1944 and he was now allowed to walk home from school along the main road with his friend George, who was ten years old.

The school was about a mile away and they had to walk up and down the hills on their way home. At the bottom of one hill on the corner of a road which came down to meet the main road there was a small grocers and greengrocers.

"That's my uncle's shop," said Barry,

George had an old stick, a branch off a tree, and was running it along a brick wall. "Will he give us some sweets?"

"Not without coupons and money."

"Will you get any sweets from Father Christmas, George?"

"Don't be daft, there ain't no such person as Father Christmas."

Barry looked at him as he was scuffing his shoe on the ground, his little shoulders hunched forward. "Yes, there is, 'cause he brings you presents," his mouth and lips beginning to drop and face going slightly red.

"Your Mum and Dad give you those and put them out while you are asleep," said George.

"You're wrong, there *is* a Father Christmas, there *is*." Barry started to cry, tears falling down his cheeks. He stamped his foot as he screamed and turned to run away crying.

of carrot, running towards them. "Cor, they look nice those big red ones. They look as if they are growing wild, they're all over the place." Barry took a big one and shoved it in his mouth.

Having had their fill, the boys began to explore the big round grey containers set in the ground which were about three foot in depth; there were four set into a square with allotments all around. Some had two arms coming out of a central pole spraying what looked like water on to this almost black semi-dry sludge as the arms spun around.

They moved to another container and leant over the side looking in.

"What are those little yellow specks in that black stuff?" said Brian.

"They are tomato pips," said a deep voice from behind them, making them both jump.

They turned and standing there was a weather-beaten man in an old grey shirt rolled up at the sleeves with brown hairy arms and a dirty cap worn away at the rim. His trousers were tied up with string and on his feet black, muddy wellington boots. Leaning against his spade he said, "What are you boys doing here?"

"We are only looking, Mister. What's this place for? I know it's called a sewage works but we don't know what it means?" said Barry.

"Well, when you have a wee and a poo it goes through a lot of pipes and ends up here. It's sprayed and dries in the sun and then I cut it up in slices and put it on the allotments," said the weather-beaten man.

"That's stinking horrid," said the boys copying each other by holding their noises. "And we have just eaten carrots and tomatoes – ugh!" said Brian holding his belly.

"Here, Mister, you said those pips were tomato seeds in the poo, do you take them out before you throw them on the allotments?" said Barry.

kept a number of tins, all with money in which she put away each week to pay the bills. Barry's Dad would give Mum his wage packet and just take out the fare to work and a small amount of pocket money. Whilst his Mum was counting out the money in the other room, Barry asked Nick, "Can I have a job helping you on your milk round, Mister?"

"You will have to get up early and you can only help me on Saturdays because you have to go to school."

"OK, how much will you pay me?"

"Wait and see if you work hard!"

"Can I start today?"

"You had better ask your Mum."

Mum had just come back to the kitchen door. "How much is it?" she asked.

"Three and six if you please, Mrs Walker. Same again next week?"

"Yes please, Nick," she said giving him a smile.

Barry, who had been standing next to his Mum, fidgeting and trying to get a word in, said, "Can I go and work for Nick, Mum?"

"What, today?"

"Yes."

"Put your coat and gloves on."

Nick had a new electric milk float which had two seats in the front cab and in the foot well was a single pedal, which when pressed moved the float forward at just faster than walking speed. Steering was by means of a half moon-shaped handle which Nick could almost lay over. On the back the milk crates were stacked: those with full milk bottles at the rear and the empties behind the cab.

Nick's round started at the Brent and continued to Swanscombe. Up and down hills, in and out of small housing estates and in wet weather the rain would blow in the open sides of the cab. In winter hands would become frozen picking up bottles covered in ice.

The year was 1947. Barry had been working for Nick for over two months. It was now late January, the snow was two to three feet thick with drifts over six feet high, it was bitterly cold. Nick and Barry had struggled, the float getting stuck and people helping and pushing to finish their round. The main road had been partly cleared and they were working their way back from Swanscombe. The road was covered in ice.

"Here, boy," Nick called out as we tried to push the float out of a drift, "you get in and steer and press down gently on the pedal while I push." Barry pulled himself by holding on to the side of the float towards the cab. His feet were freezing, and his hands were cold and covered in snow and ice even though he wore gloves. He felt very tired, but this was the first time Nick had let him drive and he was excited. They worked together as a team and slowly the vehicle began to creep up the hill.

The winter seemed to last forever, the school was closed because of the snow. Barry sat in front of the fire trying to keep warm and every few seconds scratching his feet. "Barry," his Mum shouted as she came down the stairs, "I want you to go to the shop and get some bread."

"I don't want to go, it's too cold."

"Here," said his Mum getting some coins out of her purse. "Get your coat on."

"But, Mum, my chilblains hurt, and the snow is deep!" said Barry as tears started to roll down his cheeks.

"Come on, here's your coat. Now put it on!"

It had been snowing for days; the landscape looked like fairy land with trees and houses all coated in white. Barry struggled as he tried to walk through the snow, coat pulled tight and hunched over fighting against the wind with tears rolling down his cold pink cheeks.

Arriving home freezing cold and shaking like a leaf, he ran through the back door throwing off his coat and gloves. He made a beeline for the fire, the coals glowing bright red in the grate heating the oven next to it. The stove which was made of cast iron was blacked – a bit like boot polish – by Barry's mother every day.

As he sat down his mother said, "Son, you are not going to just sit there looking at the fire, you can help me make some butter."

She held up a full bottle of milk, holding it at one end by the neck and the other by base. As she turned the bottle horizontally, she started to shake it. After some time, she passed the bottle to Barry, "Your turn." They kept this up, passing the bottle backwards and forwards until a gold-coloured plug appeared in the neck of the bottle, BUTTER!

# Chapter 7

# New House

It was nearly Spring in 1948 and the Walker family were all sitting at the table just finishing their meal. Mrs Walker started to talk, "Did you get a reply from that hospital in Sidcup, Art?"

"It came in the post today," replied Art.

"Well, what did it say?"

"I got the job."

"But does a house come with it?"

"Yes, it's in Swanley. We can catch the bus tomorrow to Dartford and then on to Swanley to have a look at it."

"When do we have to move, Dad?" asked Barry. "Do I have to go to a new school?"

Barry was talking fast, with more and more questions, getting more and more excited.

Art Walker answered his eldest son, "Slow down, yes you will have to change schools and we will be moving in about a month's time."

When the war ended, Art Walker had lost his job in Ashford, Middlesex, where he worked on tail guns for aircraft and his new job was with the new Health Service as a maintenance fitter in a laundry. Three hospitals sent their bed clothes and other items to be washed and ironed.

Some weeks later the Walker family moved. But what Barry and his parents did not know or, in the case of the parents had possible forgotten in the excitement of the move, was that Barry would miss taking his eleven plus exam.

Barry liked his new home; it had a large garden with fruit trees, plums, apples and soft fruit: red, black and white currents, and gooseberries. The house was a large end of terrace with a bathroom, a separate inside toilet and three bedrooms. Downstairs there was even a dining room!

Barry was now going to the 'big' school, as his Mum called it. But Barry was putting on weight. In fact, he was getting fat and being called names at school, fatty, bum and lots more names.

It was a mixed school with both boys and girls, with, for the want of better words, lower rough and lower middle-class pupils. Fights among the boys were commonplace at play time and after school. One day, some of the boys who seemed to be in a little gang set upon Barry, calling him names and punching him. Barry had an idea. He put his left arm across his chest and as one of the boys threw a punch, he moved the arm, so the punch landed on it and at the same time used his right arm to land a punch with his closed fist on the boy's nose. The boy started to cry.

"You hurt me," he said between sobs.

"Well don't hit me again then."

Other boys had been watching and from that day on they did not start a fight with Barry again.

Time ticked on and the kids at school began to develop. Their bodies were growing, girls started to develop larger boobs, making the boys get more excited, and they started to see hair grow around their genitals.

Barry missed having pocket money and decided to try and earn some money. He managed to get a paper round and with his Dad's help, obtained a bike. However, for Barry this was not enough, he wanted more money. Looking in one of the papers he delivered on his round, he turned to the classified advertisements and read: "Stamps on approval. We send you a book of stamps from all over the world and you can buy the stamps you would like – the prices are shown – and return the book and the stamps you don't want with your money back to us."

*What a good idea*, thought Barry, *I can up the price on each stamp, sell them to the kids and make some money.*

Little did Barry know this was his first venture into business.

Barry needed to have a wee and walked into the school toilets which were in a building out in the school yard. As he approached the boys' entrance he could hear a low moan, followed by a shout, "I win, it's just above yours!"

"Let me have a go and I'll give it a good rub."

Barry walked into the loo past the toilet cubicles to the long trough and there stood three boys with their dicks out rubbing them like mad getting them bigger and bigger, rubbing faster and FASTER! As they got to the climax, holding their penises up high, whilst moaning with their eyes half closed trying to aim their spunk higher up the wall!

Barry was in his favourite class, geography, with his favourite teacher. She was gorgeous: blue eyes, short dark hair and a small trim figure. Everyone sat in rows, the girls tending to sit together but sometimes boys would sit in with the girls trying to chat them up.

Behind Barry sat one of the boys with the girls. He was a bit rough and a bully, always picking on the smaller kids. Suddenly, Barry felt a pain in his back. He turned around and the boy had a smoker's pipe which he had unscrewed and in his hand was the metal spiral screw like those used to open wine bottles. He was jabbing it in Barry's back. "Pack that up, I'll get you outside and hit you if you don't stop it."

The boy stopped and Barry turned around to look at his teacher thinking how he would like to kiss her. He heard giggling from behind him and looked around; the girls were looking at the boy. He had his penis out and he was rubbing it to make it bigger. "Come on, girls, you can all touch it," he was saying with a glazed look on his face.

School finished for the day and Barry started to talk to Jean. She was wearing a skirt and a jumper which was a bit tight and showed off her nice-rounded boobs. "Do you want to see my bike?" said Barry pointing to the bike shed.

"It's just over there. Do you want to go behind the shed first and I'll show you something?"

"OK," said Jean skipping towards the back of the shed. "What are you going to show me," asked Jean.

"If you let me touch your boobs, I'll take out my willy to show you."

"All right," she said pulling up her jumper and showing her small, rounded breasts. Barry thought they were lovely and started to fondle them, cupping his hands around each one and slowly turning his hands forward and back.

"They feel so soft and nice."

"It's nice when you are so gentle, you can kiss my nipples if you like."

Barry bent down and pouting his lips gently kissed her nipples. His mouth was wet, and he began to dribble making her breasts wet. She started to make slight movements with her head, moving from side to side and wiggling her body. Barry started to feel a slight throbbing in his genitals and his willy started to grow bigger. Barry started to unbutton his short trousers, having taken his hands off her boobs, his penis almost fighting to get out.

Jean looked down. "Oh, that's nice; it's growing bigger! Can I touch it?"

"You can rub it if you like."

Jean moved her hand down and put her hand around the shaft, and was just starting to rub up and down when there was a lot of shouting from the other side of the bike shed. One voice was very loud, it sounded just like the Head Master! They both stopped and Jean was hurrying to pull her jumper down as Barry was trying to do up his trousers. They did not realise they were making any noise.

They heard the Head Master say, "You three boys stay there," as he came around the back of the shed, just catching Barry doing his buttons up, his penis having suddenly grown smaller.

"Your name?"

"Barry Walker, Sir."

The Head Master's face was red as he almost spat out the words, "Nine o'clock tomorrow in my office." He then turned to Jean, "You, young lady, get off home NOW!"

He grabbed Barry by the ear and began to march him round to the front of the shed where he placed Barry with the other three boys who were all now standing to attention. "All of you, in my office at nine o'clock tomorrow. Now GO!"

The next day the four boys lined up outside the Head Master's office just before 9am waiting to be called in. They all looked sheepish, their faces showing fear, and the legs were shaking of two of the boys. Whispering to each other, two others were talking in very low voices, "Do you think we'll get the cane?"

"I don't know."

Suddenly, the Head Master's door flew open; he stood there with a cold look on his face. "In here, all of you!" The boys walked in one by one.

"Stand in a line against the wall." The Head turned and grabbed his cane off the desk. The boys were all trying to look ahead and not at the cane, which he was swishing up and down against the palm of his hand.

Out of the corner of his eye, Barry could see the boy next to him shaking. Barry did not feel so good, he wished it was all over. The Head walked up and down the line, smacking his palm with the cane in front of each boy. "I should cane each one of you" – one of the boys looked as though he was going to cry – "but this time I'm going to let you all off with a warning. If I catch any of you misbehaving again you will all be back here and the lot of you will get eight strokes of the cane. NOW GO!"

# Chapter 8

# First Business

Barry was not selling many stamps and, as the school was closed at weekends, he was at a loose end after finishing his paper round even though he spent time reading most of the customers' newspapers. He was in the village one day looking at a delivery bike up against the grocer's wall and thought, *I wonder if I could get a Saturday job delivering the groceries?* As his Mum and Dad could not afford to give him pocket money, he had to try to earn money as best he could.

Barry had now found another job. Each customer had a book in which she wrote her order and Barry would deliver the groceries and collect the money every Saturday. One Saturday Barry delivered to a posh house and knocked on the back door. The door was opened by the lady of the house. "Good morning, Mrs Jones," said Barry as he handed her the cardboard box, "your groceries and your bill."

"Thank you, Barry, I'll just get the money."

Mrs Jones went back into the kitchen and returned with her purse. As she gave Barry the money, she asked him to write 'paid' in her book. Barry struggled; he had a problem with spelling. Three times he tried to spell 'paid'. In the end Mrs Jones came to his rescue and told him how to spell the word.

At that time, Barry did not realise he was partly dyslexic – sometimes being able to spell a word then a few minutes later being unable to – and when reading, putting words in or leaving them out of a text.

Life got better at school. He started to enjoy some of the lessons, with the exception of history. The teacher was so boring and would come up behind and hit you on the head with a hardback book or throw chalk at you.

One day Barry left school on his bike and cycled down the main road on his way home, he stopped and got off ready to cross the road. As he stood there waiting for a gap in the traffic so that he could cross the road, a car stopped alongside him. A man leant out of the window and Barry thought he wanted to know the way to somewhere. "Hello, do you like riding your bike?" he said.

"Yes," replied Barry.

The man continued, "Do you also like walking?"

"Sometimes."

"In the woods? Would you like to come to the woods, we can put your bike in the back?"

Barry, at this age, did not know what the man really wanted. But he replied: "No thanks, I've got to get home."

The man drove off, maybe to look for another boy?

Barry started to take more interest in school work, and this must have been noticed by his teachers for soon he became a prefect. One of his duties, with his fellow prefects, was to keep the other kids in line as they went into assembly. But still with a little bit of devil in him, he would confiscate sweets from the younger kids to share with the other prefects!

Barry was home from school and had just eaten his tea. He was reading the newspaper when his Mum turned to him, "Do they teach you about sex at school, boy?" Barry did not hear; he was too engrossed in the newspaper. She repeated the question, a little louder this time, "Do they tell you about sex at school?"

"What? Oh, you mean sex? I know all about that." This was the beginning and the end of his only sex lesson at home or at school!

Barry loved cycling and started to go out on his bike, exploring the countryside, down small lanes and finding interesting villages. His paper round was the longest the newsagent had and because of his interest in world affairs, business and travel, he would read most of the papers before delivering them which would make him late for school.

One other interest, like most boys of his age, was girls and he became very friendly with one of the girls at school and they would go for walks together. One evening when he was working on his bikes in the garden shed, his mother called out from the back door, "Your girlfriend's here."

Barry opened the shed door, "Come in, Julie."

As Julie came into the shed, Barry gave her a little kiss. They closed the door and Barry started to fondle Julie, playing with her breasts, both getting more excited, Barry could feel his penis getting hard and growing bigger. He lifted up her dress as she leaned against the shed door and tried to get her legs apart; she started to make small sounds, and he undid his fly buttons and got out his prick, rubbing it, moving his hand up and down making it hard. His breathing becoming heavy, he pushed it between her legs, trying hard to get it in her virgin parts. "Barry, Julie, are you OK out there? You had better come in!" They both gave a jump, Julie quickly pulling down her dress, Barry's willy shrinking like a deflated balloon!

Barry was coming up to fifteen years old and it was time to leave school and find a job. He had no qualifications and, because of the house move, he'd never taken the eleven plus exam, having somehow fallen through the net. His mother and father did not take much interest in his education during the war years and as far as Barry could remember they had never read to him when he was younger.

He applied for an apprenticeship at a factory in Dartford and was told he had to take an exam. Some weeks later he received a letter informing him that he had passed the exam and was offered a five-year apprenticeship from the age of sixteen as a centre lathe turner, plus one year in the offices prior to starting.

"Boy!" said his mother, addressing Barry during school holidays, "Dad and I are going to have a holiday and we are taking young Dick with us."

"Where are you going, Mum?"

"We are going to stay in a caravan in Dawlish in Devon, but there is no room for you. Will you be alright on your own?"

"Course I will."

"I'll leave you some food in the fridge; don't eat it all at once, and I'll give you some money for you to buy fish and chips. There's some milk and bread in the bread bin and there's plenty of jam. Now, you sure you will be alright?" said his Mum with a slightly worried look on her face.

"Don't worry, Mum, I'll be OK."

The day arrived and Barry helped his Dad carry the two small suitcases up the slope in front of the house to the bus stop, which was almost outside the house. His parents were to catch a train to London and then take a bus to Dawlish.

Barry was having a whale of a time eating what he liked, out training on his bikes, reading all the newspapers on his paper round and having no school. But, by the middle of the week he was getting bored.

He had joined the YHA some months ago and started to study the map showing hostels on the way to Devon. He packed some food and water together with his wet-weather gear and maps and set off for the West Country. The first day he cycled across Kent and East and West Sussex to Winchester in Hampshire on one of his bikes with a fixed seventy-eight gear and being fixed he could not free wheel but had to pedal all the time he was moving. That evening he called at the YHA and stayed the night. Next day after breakfast and completing his cleaning duties he set off for Devon.

He arrived in Dawlish in the afternoon and started to look for the caravan sites along the High Street. Looking around, there seemed to Barry that there must be hundreds of caravans and he had no idea where they would be staying. He started to ride up the hill at the end of the street and who should be coming the other way but his young brother Dick with two other boys in tow.

"What are you doing here?"

"I've come to see Mum and Dad; where is the caravan?"

"I'll show you."

Barry followed the three boys up the hill and through a gate into a large field. Barry looked around as he continued to follow, there were caravans everywhere stretching as far as he could see.

"What are you doing here, boy?" said his mother standing at the entrance to the caravan with a surprised look on her face. She was dressed in a floral frock over which was her pinny on which she was wringing her hands.

"I got bored and had eaten most of the food, so I thought I'd come down to see you."

"You didn't ride down here in one day?!"

"No, Mum, I stayed at Winchester YHA last night."

Barry stayed a few days and played games with his brother and friends, went walking down the beach and ate the food his mother cooked. He was not supposed to stay in the caravan and at night his Dad hid his bike underneath, and he slept on the floor.

Friday came and his Mum said, "We go home tomorrow, and we have to be out of the caravan by 10 in the morning. What are you doing to get home?"

"I'll leave early in the morning, Mum."

"Have you got any money?"

"I've got a shilling left," Barry said looking down at the coin he had just taken from his pocket.

"Here boy, take this ten-bob note."

His Dad was looking over his mother's shoulder. "When do you expect to get home?"

"I'm going back the other way, up to Somerset and across Salisbury Plain, so I'II be back Sunday afternoon."

Barry set off early Saturday morning on his seventy-eight fixed wheel bike. He wore his shorts and shirt with his water bottle fixed to the frame and a small amount of food that his mother had given him.

He kept going, his feet clipped to the pedals, his legs moving all the time; he could not stop moving his legs even on the downhill stretches. At Frome he stopped for a rest and to eat some of his food and whilst eating he got out his sketch pad and started to sketch the rooftops from his high point on the hill.

Soon he was off again, up the hills and down, across Salisbury Plain heading towards London. In the early- to mid-1950s there was very little traffic and no motorways on Barry's route. The weather was fine with very little wind and soon it was time for Barry to have another break. He stopped at a pub out in the country and sat just inside the bar. Having just come in from the sun, the pub appeared dark, and the floor was stone slabs polished by the locals' boots as they walked over them. There were a number of old dark wooden tables, oak beams and a big open fireplace with logs stacked on either side.

Having got his soft drink, he looked around at what appeared to young Barry to be some old farm labourers sitting talking nearby. Each had a square, checked cloth laid out on the table in front of them on which was a large lump of cheese, an onion, and a large piece of bread and at the side a pint of dark beer. Barry tried to understand what they were talking about but to him they were talking funny.

It was still Saturday and Barry kept on riding, but soon it started to get dark, and he had to put on his lights. He began to think he may make it home that night and not have to find somewhere to stay.

He knocked at the door. Slowly the door opened. "What are you doing here?" said his Dad with a surprised look on his face. "We have only just got in and you only left us this morning?"

Barry had ridden over two hundred miles in a day on a fixed wheel!

Sometimes, Barry and his mother would sit and have a chat after he had read his father's newspaper. It was on one of those days that Barry asked his mother about her brothers and sisters, of whom there were fourteen, some of which were half brothers and sisters as her mother had been married twice.

"Mum, what does Uncle George do to earn a living?"

"Well, he started off by selling rabbit skins around Dartford, from the back of his horse and cart. That's how he met your Aunt Ryar, who was a gipsy. He has done well. He now has a greengrocer's round and a shop. He's had a bungalow built with a big yard behind. The yard was made so that he could park his grocer's lorry and a gipsy caravan for Aunt Ryar's mother to live in."

"What's the caravan like?"

"It was horse drawn, made of wood and beautifully painted in green and yellow. Aunt Ryar's mother would only go as far as your aunt's kitchen to have a cup of tea, she would never go into the rest of the bungalow. When she died, they set light to the caravan; that's what the gypsies do!"

## TO WORK

# Chapter 9

# Apprenticeship

He arrived at the main gate at 7.15am having ridden his bike from Swanley. The factory gates were near the bottom of Station Approach. He had to call at the gatehouse and, having given his name, he waited in the yard until his name was called. Men were streaming through the gates: some walking, others on bikes. Behind Barry, fixed to the wall, was a large clock and on either side of the clock were a number of cards with names on, all sitting in slots. Men were removing their cards and putting them in another slot and pulling a leaver which stamped the time on the card. These were then taken out and placed back in another slot below the clock.

His name was called by a thin man holding a clip board. "Come with me, Walker, you are to work in the Post Room." As they walked across the yard, Barry looked up at the red brick building three storeys high. Scattered on the walls were pock marks made by flying shrapnel from the bombs in the war.

He was shown into a room where three girls were sorting the post and putting the letters into wooden slots. Larger items such as drawings or plans together with magazines were put into piles on a table. Barry was introduced to the head girl. "Come with me, I'll take you up to Mr Thompson's office, you are going to work with him."

They climbed the stairs to the first floor. Walking along the corridor they came to a small door. The girl knocked and opened the door and they both walked into a small room. Barry glanced around. The place looked like something from Dickens. On a high stool sat a grey-haired man. His hair was almost white which matched the hair on his top lip, and he seemed tall but as soon as he got down off the high stool, he stood no taller than Barry. His desk, which Barry later noticed, was made of large drawers containing clear linen master drawings and on the top were piles of magazines. Mr Thompson had been sticking labels on the front of magazines. On each label were a number of names and against each name were two boxes; some boxes had a tick in them, the others were empty.

"What's your name, son?"

"Barry Walker, Sir."

"Well, Barry, you are going to work for me, and you have a very important job to do," he said sniffing.

Barry noticed that the grey, almost white hair on his top lip was stained brown as were the fingers on his right hand. He was twisting each end and sniffing and there was a drop of snot on the end of his nose.

The girl had left to go back to the Post Room and Mr Thompson continued, "What you have to do is take these books and magazines around the offices every day and collect the ones that have been read. Those that have been read have been signed in this box here," he said pointing to the second box after each name.

Barry soon found his way around delivering and collecting the magazines. One day as he was coming back from his rounds and passing an open door, which he had thought was a cupboard, he looked inside. Mr Thompson was standing at a sink washing small squares of the linen drawings. Thompson had not seen Barry who carried on watching. He was rubbing the squares and screwing them up and then unfolding and laying them flat on the side. When he had a small pile, he stopped and picked them up one at a time and laid them over a string hung between two pipes to dry. *I wonder what they are for*, thought Barry. It was some days later that Barry found out as Mr Thompson took one out of his pocket to blow his nose.

One day in the Post Room, Barry started to chat up the girls and the subject got around to the exam he had to pass in order to get an apprenticeship. "I bet I had some of the top marks," Barry boasted to the girls.

"No, you didn't, you were near the bottom!"

Barry's face turned a bit grey, the faint smile replaced by dropped lips. "Was I?" he said in a gravel voice feeling choked. Barry turned and started to leave the Post Room.

As he was going out the door, he overheard one of the girls say in a quiet voice, "Bloody big head!"

Some months later Barry was sent to the Apprentice Shop to learn basic engineering skills by hand and on various machines before he was transferred to a Production Shop.

Barry was now working in the South Machine Shop and on his own allotted lathe. The so-called 'Shop' was a bit like a small aircraft hangar, with different machines either side of a wide central gangway. Strung from the roof were iron rods which held a long shaft. Along the shaft at intervals were wheels and from these wheels leather belts ran down to many of the machines to drive them by rotating the chucks which held the metal being shaped. Each operator was allocated his own machine.

Now six or seven years after the war, many of the machines had been built in the 1920s and had never been replaced.

Two foremen were in charge of the South Machine Shop. They had had an office set about ten feet up the end wall so they could see all the men working through the window. At one side, about halfway down the north wall, was a wide exit to allow goods to come in to be worked on and finished items to go out. On one side of the exit were the stores and on the other side the tool shop where special tools were made for fitting on the machines.

Along the south side was a green door which led to the lavatories, called 'the bogs' by the men. Inside were a long urinal and a series of toilets behind green doors which were cut low at the top and high off the ground so that the foreman could look over or under to see if anyone was in them for too long, reading their newspapers!

There were about twenty-five men and two apprentices working on the machines and when the foremen were missing at meetings or at the other end of the shop, then one or two of the operators would take a slip of paper and wander off around the factory for a chat. No one would challenge a person with paper in their hand thinking they were on an important mission.

There was a fifteen-minute tea break in the morning, three quarters of an hour lunch break and another fifteen-minute tea break in the afternoon. During the breaks, which were mostly taken sitting on old wooden crates, the men would talk about football and politics. Most were Labour supporters, and all wanted more money in their wage packets.

A conversation would start about big companies making lots of money and not paying their workers a reasonable wage.

"Look how much money they made," said a big guy holding up the 'Daily Worker' newspaper.

Three or four more joined in: "Yeah, they could pay us double."

"We ought to talk to the Union and get them to get us a pay rise!" The discussion started to get a bit heated.

Suddenly, Barry got up and started to say in a loud voice, "YOU DON'T KNOW WHAT YOU ARE TALKING ABOUT!" trying to make himself heard.

The talking stopped and they turned to look at this young upstart. Barry continued, "Don't you know the difference between turnover and profit? You keep on about wanting new and more up-to-date machinery. Where do you think the money's coming from?"

There was a movement behind Barry. One of the men got up and, just before picking up his wooden box, signalled with his hands to two of the others to follow him.

Still trying to explain, Barry felt his arms being grabbed at the elbows. He was lifted into the air and the men started to laugh as he was lifted up and placed on a soap box. Barry never did finish his lecture to the workers.

# Chapter 10

# The Club

Barry started to make friends with other apprentices, some of whom were into riding bikes. Others who played musical instruments had formed a band. One apprentice said to Barry, "Are you going to take the National Certificate?" Barry had not thought of taking an exam, he was into his bike races, getting up at three in the morning and cycling to the start of a race against the clock over twenty-five or fifty miles.

Barry wanted to be a draughtsman and realised he had to go to college and obtain his National Certificate, so he enrolled for evening class.

Having always liked music, Barry saved up and bought himself a clarinet and started to have lessons so that he could join his friends in their band.

He was still building bikes; he now had seven of which one was a three-wheel racing bike that he used for hill racing against the clock. He followed the band around on Saturday nights going to dances and, of course, meeting girls, but still out training on his bike at three in the morning during the week before cycling to work to be there at seven thirty, and racing early on Sunday morning, sometimes with a start time of 4am.

Something had to give and as he had not kept up his homework for the National Certificate he stopped going to classes.

Some of the cyclists got together at weekends and would go riding in the countryside. Barry, who was good at map reading and had explored many areas up to fifty or sixty miles from his home, nearly always planned the routes. One day he rode his tricycle into work and as he entered the yard the boys and men turned to look at him, some calling out, "Can't you ride a two-wheel bike yet? Get a man's bike, son."

Barry stopped near some of the apprentice lads who had been calling out. "Come on, you lot, I bet you can't ride it," said Barry getting off the tricycle.

Four lads stopped and stood looking at the bike, one turned to Barry, "How much you bet me?"

"I'll bet you six pence."

"OK," the lad said as he got on the tricycle. He started to pedal, and the bike moved off in a circle and try as he might he could not make the machine go in a straight line. "How the bloody hell do you make this thing go straight?"

Barry held his hand out, "You owe me six pence, come on pay up." The other three lads had a go at riding the tricycle but not one could ride it. *Great*, thought Barry, *I've made two bob*.

While out riding one Sunday with the lads, one of them started to talk about cycling clubs.

"Now that a few of us go out riding on a regular basis, why don't we form a club?"

"That's a good idea," said another, "but what do we call the club?"

All the riders were in agreement and a discussion took place, some of them coming up with weird names. It seemed to Barry that they were all talking at the same time. He started to shout, "STOP! All of you shut up a minute, let Peter have a say." All the talking stopped, and Peter had the floor.

"My suggestion is we call the club, Nova Astra."

"What's that mean?" said one of the others.

"It means New Star!"

"Right," said Barry looking around at them, "it sounds good to me. All those who agree that we form a club and call it Nova Astra raise your hands." All the hands went up.

Agreement having been reached, they all met in a pub some days later and after chatting to the landlord he agreed to rent them a room upstairs. They met once a month to plan their outings and to introduce new members. The club members would go on cycling trips to Norfolk, Surrey, and Sussex.

Some of the lads, including Barry, liked pubs and in the 1950s there were many in Dartford. The apprentices had a challenge. The challenge was to visit all the pubs from the top of East Hill down through the High Street finishing at the last pub at the top off West Hill, drinking a pint of beer in each. No one ever accomplished it, but there were a lot of thick heads and sick apprentices.

It was a week or two before Christmas and Barry asked his Mum if he could have a party at home with his cycling mates and one or two from work. "I'll have a word with Dad, but I would think so."

Barry invited Brian, George, Roger and Peter with his girlfriend Kim, her with lovely legs, and many more.

Telling them of the party and mentioning Kim was coming Brian said, "We should get Kim a present."

"Yeah, but what?" said one of the others.

"I know, there's a ladies shop down in the High Street, let's all go down there and see if we can find something."

The guys walked down to the High Street, chatting and laughing as they walked. The shop was at the end of a parade of five shops and its entrance was on the corner. Outside there were dresses hung on rails. The boys decided to try and buy Kim a pair of knickers but had no idea of what size.

"Ere, who's going to go in and buy them? I can't see any in the window; I bet they don't sell them." George was getting cold feet and was starting to look a little scared as he held back from the door.

"Don't be daft, it's a ladies shop, they must sell them. Let's go in and ask," said Barry as he turned to walk in the shop. Barry turned again to look at the guys who were hiding behind the rack of ladies' dresses, laughing and trying to push each other to go in.

"You go first."

"No, you go."

*Oh bugger it*, thought Barry and walked up to a shop assistant.

The shop assistant looked at Barry with a grin on her face. To Barry she seemed old, perhaps in her thirties. "What can I do for you, young man?" she said grinning.

"I, um, was looking for, um, a present for my girlfriend."

"Would you like to see some jumpers?"

"Well, I was thinking of, um, some knickers," he said, blushing as he heard the tittering in the background.

"What size is she?"

Bloody hell thought Barry, I haven't got a clue. "I, um, don't know."

"Well, is she big around the hips?"

Barry, still feeling embarrassed and his face slightly red, thought, *how can I give a size?*

"Well, they're about this wide." Barry held out his hands in front of him with his palms facing each other.

"How tall is she?"

"Oh, she's only short, about so high," he said holding one hand up to his chest.

"What colour would you like?" the assistant said, holding up a pink pair of knickers.

"Have you got them in pale blue?" Barry was beginning to feel more comfortable.

Barry had the knickers wrapped, paid for his purchase, turned and left the shop, meeting the guys outside. They were all chatting away behind the rack of dresses.

"How did you get on? Did you get some? Let's have a look. What colour are they?" They were all trying to talk at the same time.

"Did you get ETBs?"

"What are ETBs?"

"Don't you know!"

Barry looked at George. "It means elastic top and bottom, and no I didn't get them. They're finger catchers."

"Chance would be a fine thing," and they all started to laugh as they were thinking how nice it would be if they could only try.

"You all owe me your share of the cost before you can see them," said Barry, putting his hand out for the money. Everyone paid up and turned to Barry, waiting for him to unwrap the knickers.

"No, I'm not going to unwrap them, Kim will have to show you when we give them to her at the party."

The party started with a swing. Barry had invited some friends from the cycling club and some from work. His Mum and Dad were nowhere to be seen! Music on the gramophone was playing some of the latest songs. Girls were trying to dance, and the lads were drinking and telling dirty jokes when Barry gave a shout.

"Time, girls and boys, for those who have brought presents to give them to their best friends. To start it off, my gang of friends would like to give Kim a present, from us. Happy Christmas, Kim."

Kim came over to the boys looking gorgeous. She was beauty in miniature, a perfect figure with her slim waist and, although they could not see them, her lovely slim legs. She was smiling as she stood in front of Barry, smelling so nice that Barry could have eaten her. Unfortunately, her boyfriend Peter stood beside Kim giving Barry and the others a glowering look.

"Kim, this is from all of us, but not from Peter as I'm sure he has got you a present."

As she unfolded the paper the boys – almost all at the same time – said, "Let's see."

Kim held up the knickers as the others who had been dancing and drinking stopped to look. "Thank you," she said smiling.

Peter and Kim went out into the kitchen, the others back to their drinking and dancing. Some minutes later the kitchen door opened, and Peter came out. "George, come with me," he said as he turned taking him into the room.

George came out grinning a few minutes later. "Cor, your turn, Barry!" Barry almost ran into the kitchen.

"Close the door," said Peter standing in front of Kim. He moved away and there stood Kim holding up her dress high above her waist showing her knickers and those lovely legs. Barry could not help staring, a look of lust on his face, almost dribbling at the mouth, trying to control his hands which seemed to have a life of their own as they wanted to touch this beautiful girl and pull her to his side.

"Do you like them?"

"Like them! Bloody hell, you must be joking. It's you that's lovely."

The party started to get more boisterous, the lads playing tricks on each other with one or two of the girls joining in. Barry and Brian were laughing as they were being chased around the front room into the kitchen and back, they flew out the front door on to the drive.

"It's bloody cold out here," Brian said, shivering in his shirt and jumping up and down trying to keep warm. "It's bloody dark, too. Come on, try the door."

The front door was shut. They knocked and banged with their fists getting more and more frustrated. They started to shout, "LET US IN, IT'S COLD OUT HERE!"

"It's no good, they are not going to let us in." Barry was shivering, his teeth chattering. "Let's see if we can find another way in," he said as he started to look around.

Brian was looking up at the upstairs windows. "Look, that window seems to be open."

"That's my bedroom window, we could get in there."

"But how are we going to get up there, we need a ladder."

Barry thought for a moment as he stood there shivering. "I know where a ladder is, there's one a few doors down in the back garden."

Brian followed Barry. "Be quiet, we have got to go around the side and borrow it without them knowing."

They crept along the tarmac drive which stretched in front of the houses.

"What if he comes out?"

"We run, you silly bastard, now be quiet."

"Oh shit, I hit my toe," said Brian dancing on one leg.

"Shut up!"

It was almost pitch black as they crept around the back of the house. "There it is," whispered Barry, "you get one end and I'll take the front." They picked up the ladder trying not to make a noise as they crept back. Still shivering, they stopped in front of the house and looked up, the window was still open. Huffing and puffing they placed the top of the ladder just under the open window. The music and laughter were getting louder.

"They won't be able to hear us, I'll go up first," said Barry. "You follow me up." Barry started up the ladder with Brian following two steps behind. They were nearly at the top when the window flew open and a bucket full of water, soaked Barry, who nearly fell off the ladder. The ladder started to wobble. Brian had never come down a ladder so fast. He was spluttering, and just managed to get off before the ladder started to slide to one side.

A shout went up amid the laughter from those looking out of the window: "GOTCHA!"

It was New Year, and the apprentices were back at work; they were now earning over six or seven pounds per week with overtime. One afternoon, as they sat on their boxes having a tea break, the conversation got around to holidays. Most suggested seaside towns such as Margate, Brighton, and Blackpool. Barry suddenly had an idea, "Let's go abroad somewhere."

"But none of us speaks any foreign languages."

"Well, we could go to one of the Channel Isles."

The die was set. They all agreed they would go to Jersey and Barry was given the job of finding out the cost.

It would take eight or more hours, subject to the weather, to reach Jersey on the overnight ferry. They were all a little apprehensive, this being their first trip abroad. They only had chairs to sleep in so for most of the night they propped up the bar drinking. After a while, some of the five decided to try and get some sleep. The ship was rolling and crashing into waves in the rough sea. Those still standing did a comical dance away from and back towards the bar, trying not to spill their drinks.

Barry needed some fresh air: "I'm going on deck."

"It's dark out there, don't fall over the side!"

Barry leant over the rail looking between the life boats at the waves and the white horses, the ship rolling up and down and crashing into the waves making her pitch up at the bow, the sea water rising high over the lower decks and splashing down like a waterfall. On the upper deck, Barry looked around. A few people were lying on the deck wrapped in blankets trying to get some sleep. The door opened behind him, and a chap rushed to the rail next to Barry. He leant over and made a terrible noise. Barry could hear it coming up, and suddenly he was very sick over the side, just missing Barry.

Barry felt funny, he had a grumbling noise coming from down below. Feeling hot, light-headed and rough, it was Barry's turn to feed the fish beer and partly digested food.

At last, they reached Jersey. The boys stood on the deck watching the ship sail slowly into the harbour.

"Look at that, over there."

"What?"

"On the wall, that sign, 'Try Mary Ann!'"

"Bloody hell, are they advertising prostitutes?"

"Don't know, we'll have to find out."

They carried their cases off the ferry and found the bed and breakfast lodging. They had all agreed to take their dark blue blazers and grey trousers to go out in the evening and once settled in, they went out to find a pub or bar in their smart clothes.

Barry looked around as they walked through the streets. "I've just found out that Mary Ann is a beer!"

The other boys looked at him. "What!" they all said.

"Look over there," said Barry pointing. "On the window of that pub, it's a type of beer."

They found a nice-looking cocktail bar and decided to go in. The place was decorated in the latest fashion with a bar at one end and high stools around it. Over the back of the bar there were rows of optics and one row had ten bottles of Pimms, all different colours and numbered one to ten.

Barry looked at the bar, "Let's sit on the stools at the bar and try some of those Pimms. Let's start at number one and see if we like it; if we do, we can try the next number."

They had completely forgotten about food and by the time they had finished number ten they were all pissed.

Next day after breakfast and looking a little worse for wear, they went to search for a bike shop to hire tandems to explore the isle.

# Chapter 11

# Outings

Tea break at work is the time when everyone catches up with the news, dates to meet are agreed, places to go are arranged, pubs to visit are discussed, and dirty jokes are shared. A chap that Barry did not know very well suggested they "go up town", meaning London. Barry agreed and arranged to meet at Dartford Station on Saturday afternoon to travel to Charing Cross. They walked around the West End looking at the sites and calling at a number of pubs. The Strand, Trafalgar Square, Soho, looking at the sex clubs with bouncers on the doors and watching the prostitutes trying to obtain trade from some of the men. They could hear music and singing coming from inside some of the pubs. Barry and his friend found it very exciting with the noise, coloured lights and the people.

Time was ticking on, but the lads had not noticed, they were too interested in what was going on around them. Sometime later they found themselves in Shaftsbury Avenue, which was far quieter than Soho. Black London taxis were parked in the centre of the road facing towards Piccadilly. Along the side of the avenue standing in doorways were the prostitutes plying for trade. Barry's mate went up to one trying to chat her up. "How much?" he said.

"Ten bob, and you pay the taxi fare."

They went on walking towards Piccadilly watching the men who went in the taxis with the girls. It seemed they were only gone around the block for a few minutes. As they watched, the taxis had hardly moved away before the back seemed to be bouncing.

Sometime later Barry was watching the people in Piccadilly, and he turned to talk to his friend, but he had disappeared. He waited a while and then thought to himself, *I bet he's gone with a prostitute. I had best go and catch the last train home.*

As he went to leave, he walked past a smart fat man in a suit who was talking to a boy, who must have been about 12 or 13 years old. "Would you like to come home with me?" he heard the man say. Barry wondered what a boy of that age was doing at that time of night and why the man was offering to take him home. It seemed a bit like the man who had wanted to take Barry to the woods.

Barry got to the station, but it seemed almost empty, looking around he could only see the old tramps sleeping on the benches. He looked up at the timetable board. *Bloody hell*, he thought, *the next train is not till 5.00 am, what am I going to do now?*

Barry left the station and walked down towards the Thames. He turned to the left and walked along the embankment. Just past the Underground at the end of the building set in a small square a fire was burning, the fire was made of old wooden boxes. Sitting on boxes were a number of rough looking individuals, all of whom were dressed in dirty old clothes. Some were thin women; their drawn faces all white, puffing on fags and coughing. Others were holding mugs of tea with their filthy hands trying to keep warm. To one side stood a dirty white catering van, its lid up and the fat man standing inside handed a mug of tea to another tramp.

Barry stood unnoticed by the tramps as he watched the fire and then suddenly became aware of someone walking towards him from his left.

He turned to see a Teddy boy in his fashionable suit with the jacket buttoned up to the neck, black velvet lapels and collar. Hanging from one corner of his mouth was a cigarette stuck to his lip; the other corner of his lip was cut and slit half away down to his cheek and covered in congealed blood. Obviously, he had been in a fight involving knives.

Feeling just a little frightened, Barry decided it was time to leave but as there were no trains or buses going his way, he had to walk. Crossing the river, he started to walk to Waterloo past the station and on towards the Elephant and Castle. There was very little traffic and just the occasional homeless person asleep under cardboard boxes in a doorway. From time to time a taxi would pass by with its light turned off as the driver was on his way home. Barry thought about trying to stop one to get a lift but not having much money left he decided to walk.

After many miles walking through South London and into Kent he arrived at Sidcup. Walking through the High Street an early bus passed by. *Maybe there is an early one going to Swanley*, he thought. After a wait of twenty minutes or so he caught one going to Swanley. Arriving home, he turned the key in the door just as his father was coming down the stairs. "Morning, Pop," he said as he waited for him to get down the stairs so he could go up to bed.

Barry was coming up to his 19th birthday and was looking for more adventure. He decided to sell his bikes and buy a car but there was a problem. Even after selling all six bikes and his one tricycle he would not have sufficient money to buy a car. He asked his parents if they could lend him some money, but they said they could not afford to lend him any and suggested he ask his aunt, who said she would lend him the money, on condition that he repaid her weekly from his wages.

Barry applied for a provisional licence and found his first car, a 1937 Morris Ten, made in the year Barry was born. The car was a heavy old thing, built on an iron chassis. The boot – or trunk, as the Americans call it – could only be accessed by folding down the back seat. The indicators were two little arms in yellow just like butterfly wings which sprang out each side of the car at the door posts between the back and front doors. Inside the seats were covered in leather and the doors, by today's standards, opened the wrong way so you had to close the doors before moving or the doors could rip off. But being an upmarket second-hand model it had the luxury of air conditioning: a sliding sun roof!

After two attempts, Barry passed his driving test. The bikes had gone, and all his mates wanted to know him to try and get lifts!

Barry's gang – Brian, Roger and the others – five altogether, went for an early evening drive in the country and, as always, ended up in a pub. They left just before closing time having drunk a few pints of beer each. Getting into the car they started to sing, and Roger got out his mouth organ and began to play.

"It's hot in here, open the sun roof," someone said.

Roger stood up on the front seat, his head and shoulders out of the top of the car. They were all laughing, Brian trying to pull Roger's trousers down whilst he was trying to play. Barry, his confidence in his driving increased by the drink, was driving a little too fast around the lanes. They turned down a narrow lane which had high earth banks on each side. The road surface had just been improved with tar and gravel. Suddenly they came to a sharp bend. Barry braked hard – the car started to slide, and he could not control it. *CRASH!* The car hit a bank.

Roger made a funny noise, and Barry tried to look at the same time as he hit the steering wheel with his chin. Roger had stopped playing, the engine had stopped, and Barry flew forward and hit his head. The three in the back had all shot forward.

"Shit, that hurt!" The doors flew open and half crawling, holding on to the open doors with one hand and their heads or chests with the other, all five managed to crawl out.

It was now getting quite dark and having all got out of the car they stood talking. Brian turned to Barry, "You're bleeding, let's have a look."

Barry put his hand up to his face which felt wet. "That's nothing, I'll be alright."

They pulled the car out of the earth bank and after a discussion began to push the car up a slight slope along the lane. Brian, who was short and fat, almost like a barrel, was puffing and panting and called out, "Stop a minute, I need a rest."

They all began to move away from the car as Barry made a grab for the driver's side door handle and just managed to open the door, put his arm in, and pull up the hand break. Barry turned to the others, "Come on, just one more big push and she will be on the top lane."

They tried again and red faced, huffing and puffing, they managed to get the car to the top of the lane just as a Charabanc, an old coach, came along the road. It slowed and then stopped right in front of Barry. He looked up to see old ladies looking out of the windows of the red and cream-coloured coach. The door started to open, and he could hear some of the old ladies.

"My god, look at his face! The blood, it's all down him."

Barry wondered what they were on about. As the driver of the charabanc got out, he asked, "What's happened, son?"

Barry started to explain, but the driver interrupted: "Let's look at your face. Come on, we are going to get you to hospital, get on the coach."

Barry did as he was told and got on the coach to be greeted by the ladies, some putting their hands over their mouths, some looking very worried and others saying, "You poor lad." They carried on chatting all the way to the hospital, making comments, offering advice and starting their conversations with, "I remember when…"

At last Barry arrived at the hospital and was shown into what is now called the Accident and Emergency Department. He felt worse with all those old ladies worrying about him. A nurse came along and took him into a side room, told him to lie down on the bed and began to gently clean him up. She looked lovely in her uniform with her starched white hat, all of which was spotless and clean. As she bent her head over to clean his face, Barry thought how nice she smelled. Looking at her he was already beginning to feel a lot better!

"You are lovely and very beautiful."

The nurse began to smile, still wiping away the dried blood.

"You are going to have to have some stitches in that cut."

Barry felt as though he was in seventh heaven as he looked up into her lovely pale blue eyes, her cream smooth skin and full lips smiling at him, showing her white teeth. The wings of her white hat made her look like an angel.

"How about a date? Fancy coming out one evening?"

The nurse just smiled and did not answer.

Barry still has the scar today.

# Chapter 12

# Austria

The band had just finished playing at the Co-op Hall and some of them went back to Brian's house to have a chat and a drink. The subject got around to holidays.

"I've always wanted to go to Austria, with the mountains, flowers and the girls in their dirndls."

"What's a dirndl?"

"You know those dresses which go in at the waist and push up the boobs."

"Cor, I fancy that."

They all agreed to go to Austria, but how to get there? Barry was given the job to find the hotel and the means to get there. Another meeting was arranged over a few beers in the pub to discuss the arrangements and costs.

"OK, I've got the details. We are going by train through Northern France, Belgium and Germany to Austria. When we get to Innsbruck, we have to catch a bus to the hotel in Igls, where we can have two rooms."

They all agreed, and bookings were made. The time came to board the train carrying their cases. The gang were all excited, this being their first time on mainland Europe and were chattering away like little old hens but with deeper voices. They were all dressed in their blazers, white shirts and ties and looked very smart. Knowing the journey was going to be very long, they took sandwiches and other food to eat on the way.

Being only eleven years after the war, they were still surprised to see the devastation through the train windows. The train rattled on and stopped at the frontier station, guards getting on and checking their tickets and passports.

Somewhere in Germany the train stopped at a station to have another train connected for the onward journey and, looking out of the window, they could see a woman with a cart selling sausages and bread rolls.

Brian with his mouth watering, always the one to be hungry, said, "Let's get out and buy some of those sausages."

"But we can't speak German."

"We don't have to, we can point."

They all got off the train and stood looking at the food, pointing and trying to work out the money to pay. "Look at the size of that sausage," said Roger pointing at Brian trying to eat one he had put between a bread roll. The ends of the sausage stuck out of each side of the roll by as much again in length!

Brian wiped his chops and said, "I need the bog, do you know where they are?"

"I don't know, let's look down here," said Barry pointing to the stairs going down from the platform.

As they ran down the steps people were coming up to catch their trains. "We had better hurry in case we miss the train," said Peter.

The area at the bottom of the steps was a wide passage and the boys started to look for the loos. To the right they could see two doors. "Which one is the men's, Damen or Herren?"

"I don't know."

"It's Damen," said Peter.

Brian went up to the door and grabbed hold of the handle; he started to pull but the door did not move. He tried with both hands, leaning back to give it an almighty pull. The other boys stood watching, all of them grinning. Suddenly, Brian let go and the door flew open inwards and standing there was one of the biggest German women the boys had seen. She had a look on her red face that could kill any man and her arms were like tree trunks. Brian stood there with his mouth open, blushing like mad as he cowed back. The woman walked out in a huff just as the boys fell about laughing. They had now found out which was the gents.

On arrival at Innsbruck, they hired a car and as only Barry had a licence all the driving was down to him. With his love of maps Barry had purchased a large-scale map of Austria and plotted the route to the hotel. It was the first time Barry had driven on the other side of the road but because the driving seat was on the outside near the centre of the road, he only had to get used to changing gear with his right hand and where all the controls were.

They started to climb up the hills out of Innsbruck. The road started to get narrower, and the boys were quiet as the road started to wind upwards with the mountains in the distance and a shear drop on one side of the road. Barry looked into his rear mirror; one of the lads was gripping the back of his seat and they all looked scared. The talking had stopped and the face of one had turned white.

At last, the road evened out with green fields on each side and in the distance fir trees climbing up the lower slopes of the mountains. Barry slowed the car as there were no other vehicles around and they were all looking at the view. All different shades of green and just peeping through the trees on their left the shimming blue of a mountain lake.

Barry started off again. He drove around the slight bend past the trees to see a large building four storeys high, the top storey having a sloping roof, and each floor – with the exception of the top floor – had a wooden balcony. All around the balconies were beautiful red flowers all in different shades of red. Looking up the roof had wooden tiles coloured dark and light brown with a series of dormer windows looking out onto the mountains. At the back of the building as the roof sloped down to the top balcony, was fixed a large vertical neon sign which, the lads later discovered, was lit at night and could be seen in the valley below.

They pulled into the side of the hotel and after checking in at reception, were shown to their rooms on the top floor at the back of the building. Their rooms were next to each other, two to a room with the windows overlooking the lake they had seen earlier and the valley with Innsbruck in the distance.

That evening, having had a little too much beer and wine before and after dinner, they made their way up the stairs to bed singing and joking, their voices slurred. Brian tried to step over the top step on the third floor his feet flying up, nearly knocking out Peter, he landed face down as he slurred, "Oh shit, son." He lay there as they were all laughing. Brian, his right eye almost level with the carpet, looked along the corridor, "'ere, there's shoes," he tried to say, "let's move them."

Having at last got to the top of the stairs, the rest of them looked around. Outside each bedroom door were one or two sets of shoes, some ladies, others gents, all waiting for the night porter to clean them ready for tomorrow. The lads began to pick them up and throw them to each other, eventually placing the shoes outside the wrong doors.

Finally, getting back to their rooms on the top floor, they were too excited to sleep, and Brian said to Barry, "Open the window, it's hot in here. See if they have their window open." Barry duly conformed and opened the window and looking to his left he could see an open window to the other room. He picked up a chair and placed it under the open window and climbed up and out on to the tiled wooden roof. "Where the hell are you going!" shouted Brian.

"I'm trying to get in their room and frighten the life out of them."

"Don't be daft, there's a bloody great drop, you could kill yourself. Not only that, there's the electricity from the neon sign."

Brian looked out the window and could see the backside of Barry on the sloping roof just above the neon sign. Suddenly, a tile came loose, and Barry slid down gaining momentum and crashing over the edge, hitting the ground four floors down. Brian was sobering up fast as he watched Barry who was half crawling, half walking across the roof, his body highlighted by the neon sign. Suddenly, he reached the open window and giving a loud shout of "GERONIMO", Barry dived head first into the room. There was an almighty crash, screaming and loads of laughter. Someone shouted. "You silly bugger, you frightened the life out of me. Get him, boys!"

Brian decided to try and go to sleep and leave them to it.

# Chapter 13

# Life and Death

Barry was still following the band to various gigs in Kent with Brian as leader. In addition to playing the piano, Brian also played the piano accordion. As Barry was the only one to have a car, he was always being asked to run people around. At work one day the apprentices were asked if they would take some children's Christmas presents to the local hospital.

The day came and they loaded up the presents in Barry's car – Brian taking his accordion – and set off to the local hospital. On arrival they were shown to an area just outside the ward where a nurse in her very attractive blue uniform with white starched cuffs and hat told the lads which present to give to which child. She also told them to try and act normally as what the lads were about to see may be very upsetting. Brian asked if he could play his accordion and the nurse said that it would be a good idea. As she held the handle to the door to the ward, she said, "Let's go in."

Brian began to play as the three walked in carrying the presents of different shapes and sizes. The ward was decorated with coloured paper chains in blue, green, red and pink and in the far corner sat a small Christmas tree in a pot, on the top of which was a small angel with silver wings. The rest of the tree had little bows in various colours tied to the small branches. There were eight children of various ages, most of them in bed with two sitting in chairs beside of their beds.

Barry walked up to the first bed on his left to what looked like a man who was sitting propped up against the pillows. Barry was thinking, *I thought this was a children's ward.*

"Hello, how old are you?"

"I'm sixteen," came the reply. Barry looked down at the boy's large shoulders and chest and thought he looked like a twenty-eight-year-old weight lifter.

"I've got you a Christmas present. Happy Christmas," said Barry. The boy smiled and took the present placing it down on the bed in front of him. Barry looked down where he had put the present and suddenly realised the boy only had very tiny legs, no bigger than a three-year-old baby.

Barry started to choke up and could hardly speak and had to turn away as the lad said, "Thanks, and a Merry Christmas to you."

Still feeling emotional and trying hard to hold back the tears, Barry walked across to the other side of the ward where a small boy was sitting in a chair next to his bed. Brian was still playing Christmas carols on his accordion and some of the nurses were trying to get the children singing.

"Hello," said Barry. As he tried to find a present, he looked down at the boy. "How old are you?"

"Ten," said a tiny voice. *God*, thought Barry, *he only looks about four or five, but his skin is all wrinkled like an old man's.* Barry laid the parcel on the boy's lap as he became more choked up.

The boy slowly raised his hands to try to undo the string around the parcel and Barry bent down to try to help him. "STOP!" a nurse came up and pushed Barry's hand away. "Leave him to try by himself."

Barry just had to get out of the ward; he hurried out, and once outside the building he burst into tears, his chest heaving and sobs coming thick and fast.

The lads were talking about their grandparents and how often each had seen them in the last few months and Barry thought about his grandmother – his Mum's mother – who was now in her nineties and lived alone. She had outlived two husbands and two 'boy' friends and had borne fourteen children. Having come from a poor family, some of the children would go bare foot until one of the older children passed down their shoes. Not always at school but out trying to find a job to earn some money, most had nits and when they did get to school 'Nitty Nora', as she was called by the kids, would apply her comb and comb out as many as possible on to paper. She was not very gentle and would pull on their hair making the kids scream.

Barry's mother, Dot, remembered going hop picking at Yalding with her mother, brothers and sisters and how they lived in a wooden hut with no toilet or bath and all sleeping together 'top to tail'. The toilet was in another hut which was used by all the hop pickers and their children.

The huts were a row of terraces and the families cooked outside over wood fires. Dot also remembered Friday evenings when they were paid, and all the families would go down to the pub. The kids were all given soft drinks and would play outside while the grown-ups sang along to the songs played on the piano.

Listening to the lads talking about their grandparents, Barry had an idea: *What if some of us took my grandmother back to the pub in Yalding?* "Brian," he called out, "fancy a trip to Yalding?"

"To a pub?"

"Why else?"

After picking up Brian and George, Barry called at the little terrace house to collect his grandma. He had told her to be ready for him to take her out for the day but did not tell her where they were going. She was sitting in her chair which was padded with extra blankets over the back. She was dressed in a frock which covered her ankles and black coat. Her hair was done up in a bun and on her head a black straw hat, with what looked like fruit on the brim, sat over her grey hair. She was very short, looking like a little dumpling wrapped up in a pudding cloth.

As they arrived in Yalding, Barry said to his grandmother, who was short sighted, "Can you remember which pub you went in when you were hop picking, Gran?"

Gran looked out of the car window, squinting as she tried to see. "There it is, that one there," she said pointing, "it's not changed much."

Barry parked the car at the side of the pub and the lads opened the door for Gran helping her into the public bar. It reminded Barry of the old ''spit and sawdust'' pubs in the old days. Up against one wall was an old upright, 'Joanna', the cockney name for a piano. It was a bit battered but as Brian tried it out it was still in tune. Barry went to the bar and ordered a milk stout for his grandmother.

They all started to sing as Gran led with *Down at the Old Bull and Bush*, *Lambeth Walk* and *A Bicycle Made For Two*.

"Let's sing the *other* words to that," said Barry. With the exception of Gran, they all began to sing:

"Daisy, Daisy, the Coppers are after you,

If they catch you they'll give you a year or two,

They'll tie you up with wire behind a Black Maria,

So ring your bell and peddle like hell on a bicycle made for two."

Gran started to laugh as she joined in, and Brian stopped playing as she began to sing:

"You can't get many pimples on a pound of pickled pork,

Whether you go to China, Japan or Carolina,

You can go to Pimlico, Chicago or New York,

But you can't get many pimples on a pound of pickled pork."

On the way back to her home, Gran, when she was not singing, thanked everyone for one of her best days out ever.

She died two days later.

# GROWING UP

# Chapter 14

# National Service

Barry was nearing the end of his apprenticeship and at age twenty-one he would have to serve two years National Service or go into the Merchant Navy for five years. He had left school at fifteen, completed one year in the engineering office and five years as an apprentice. He was not looking forward to another five years being tied to the mast, as it were, even though he wanted to see the world. Two years in the Army would mean that he would be out at twenty-three.

One day, having arrived home from work, his Mum said, "There's a letter for you, boy." Barry looked at the *On His Majesty's Service* postmark and opened the brown envelope, a sick feeling starting in his stomach.

"What is it?"

"Wait, Mum, let me read it." Barry read the letter and told his mother that he had to attend a medical at Blackheath in South London.

The day came and he travelled to the Medical Centre, which was a red brick building at the top of a hill. As he approached, he could see young men going in the double doors. He walked in to be greeted by a chap sitting behind a desk.

"Name?"

"Barry Walker."

"Go through that door," said the man behind the desk, pointing to a dark brown door, "... and take off your clothes and shoes, just leave your pants and socks on. Hang your clothes on a peg."

Barry walked into the room which turned out to be long and narrow with pegs on the brown walls and two long bench seats one either side. There were three chaps in different states of undress talking in cockney accents.

"Yeah, just pretend you don't 'ear them," said one.

"My mate said they put you in a soundproof room."

"I'm going to be deaf."

"'Ere, mate, you going to give it a try?" said another looking at Barry.

"I don't know, I'll wait and see."

A man in a white coat popped his head around the opening into the medical examination room and called out the name of the chap who was going to pretend to be deaf. The lad got up and followed the white coated man.

Soon it was Barry's turn and having been called he walked in his Y-front pants and short socks to be greeted by a chap wearing a white coat sitting behind a desk. The chap did not look up from his writing but thrust out his arm with a bottle in his hand. "Go over to that sink and piss in the bottle," he said.

Barry took the bottle and turned around looking for the sink. It was set against the back wall and on the floor in front red tiles were laid, stretching almost back to the chap's desk. Getting to the sink he took out his willy and flopped it over the sink and placed the bottle under. Barry was starting to feel relieved as he had needed a pee.

"Come on hurry up, I haven't got all day," said the white coated chap.

Barry tried to stop but he was still peeing away.

"Bloody well get over here!"

Barry started to try and hold his pee at the same time as shaking his willy. He turned around holding the bottle in one hand and trying to tuck his willy back in his pants. He looked down to see drips across the red tiled floor.

The chap in white went red in the face, stood up nearly knocking over the desk and made a grab for the bottle.

"Get the f**k out of here! I've got to clean up your mess, you waste of space!" he exclaimed.

Barry turned and looked around the room, which was the size of a small village hall. He noticed there were large cubicles set against the walls and open to the centre. The lads he had met in the changing room were moving in and out of each cubicle. The next one he was about to go into was enclosed and had glass windows which were partly obscure. Barry was just about to knock on the door to enter when a very loud voice rang out.

"Get out! There's nothing wrong with your hearing, sonny! I've seen it all before. Now get out!"

*Well, that idea didn't work,* thought Barry.

After he came out of the hearing test, Barry turned to go into the next cubicle and was greeted by the sight of the back of a rather fat man, who he assumed was a Doctor, sitting at an old-fashioned roll top desk. Without turning around the Doctor said as he was writing, "Turn around and drop your pants down and bend over."

Barry did as he was told even though he felt a little nervous. He heard the Doctor scrape his chair as he got up as he was still bending over.

"Have I seen you some where before?"

Barry pulled his pants up as quickly as possible, thinking he had been looking up too many arses.

Moving on to the next cubicle he had to lie down on a bed whilst one of the white coats ran a stick over his stomach making it wobble like jelly and then tickling his feet with the same stick.

The last cubicle was different. Three men, who Barry assumed were Doctors, sat behind a table each looking at forms. He was told to sit down on a chair in front of them and they all started to ask him questions. Did he feel well? Was his left arm all OK? Did it give him any pain? Barry answered, "Yes, I feel well and no, I don't have any pain."

It was many years later when he was married and had a daughter in her twenties that he understood why they asked all those questions about his left arm.

As the train swayed and rattled, Barry stood in the corridor looking out of the window. He was looking at, but not seeing, the countryside as it flashed by, thinking about the girl he had left behind. In his mind's eye he could see her fair skin and lovely blue eyes that matched her blue dress and white petticoat as he hugged her slim figure and how she moved and swayed as she walked towards him. Tears started to well up in his eyes. "Excuse me, mate," a voice brought him out of his thoughts. Barry turned to let the chap by and noticed he was about the same age. "You going to Malvern?" he said.

"Yeah, you as well?"

"Yes."

They continued talking as the train travelled on to Malvern. They were joining the Royal Engineers and were about to start their basic training which would last six weeks.

They learned how to make beds with hospital corners and bull boots, taking the pimples out of the toes and heals with a hot iron or a spoon heated on the underside and rubbed over the pimples to flatten them. They would then cover the boots in black polish, rubbing in circles on toes and heals in layers and layers, occasionally spitting on the boots and rubbing it in. Most had an idea how to march but there were many, including Barry, who did not seem to know their left from their right foot. There were others who would bring their arm up with the same leg as they marched instead of with the opposite leg.

Barry said to the chap in the next bed, "My feet are hurting like mad."

"Piss in your boots and leave them under your pit (bed) every night until they fit," said Barry.

Barry thought he would try it that night and after peeing in his boots, he placed them under his bed. The smell started to make him feel a bit sick after the third night and he was starting to get fed up with putting on wet boots every morning, but the leather was now getting soft, and they were fitting around his feet – bliss!

One day all the recruits were all lined up, marched to a hut and told to get in single file. The door of the hut was open and the chaps at the front could see fellows in white coats moving two tables to face the door. The tables were then moved apart to leave a gap sufficiently wide for a man to walk through.

"'Ere, what's going on, Charlie?"

"Dunno, I fink they are going to examine us."

"Wot, we've all 'ad our medicals."

The third recruit from the front, his eyes staring and face turning white, was looking in the door. "I think we are going to have injections," he said, his voice shaking. "I'm not going first." The others at the front all looked a bit nervous.

"I'll go first," said Barry as he moved to the front and looked in.

There were four men in white coats and at that moment two walked out with cotton wool in one hand and a brown looking bottle in the other.

"Roll up your sleeves," the NCO shouted and as they were doing so, he shouted, "Higher!"

The men in white coats went down the line of Sappers, one on each side, tipping some liquid on to the cotton wool then wiping it on the top of the recruits' arms. A shout went up from the NCO, "From the front, move into the Medical Centre." Barry walked into the hut and was told to move between the two tables, on each side of which stood a white coat, each holding a syringe. They both got hold of an arm; the one on the right injected and the one on the left made a number of punches with his syringe. Barry was then told to go out the back door which stood open in front of him. He walked out and stood looking back at the line of men filing through; he was waiting for his mate. Tom was six feet three inches and built like a shit house door. At last, he came through, his face looking very white and swaying from side to side. Suddenly, he fainted, face down on to the hard-packed earth.

"Pick that man up and take him back to the billet!" came the shout.

Barry tried to pick Tom up but there was no way he could carry him. Others, seeing what was going on, grabbed a leg or an arm and four of them carried Tony back to the billet and laid him on his pit. Someone said, "The bigger they are, the harder they fall!"

It did not take long for the conveyor belt system to finish injecting and they were all back in the billet, some rubbing their arms, others looking a bit grey, and they all flopped on to their beds. The door suddenly flew open, and a shout went up, "Stand by your beds!"

Some moved fast, others a bit more slowly as though they were feeling ill. "Move your bloody selves, you're not dead yet! Right, you will all take turns on the bumper and swing it up and down the floor." He was referring to a long-handled pole with a large heavy wooden block on the end and a soft pad on the underside which was used to polish the centre of the floor. "Get on with it!" he shouted as he turned and walked out the door.

Someone picked up the bumper and started to swing it up and down the floor using his injected arm. After doing this a few times and feeling knackered, he handed it to another Sapper. Most of the recruits just lay on their pits reading, scratching or dozing.

"I am not doing that," said one pointing to the bumper.

"Nor me," said another.

A few moments later, one of the bodies lying on his pit said, "I feel funny and hot."

"Who you got the hots for, cos you ain't getting any in here!"

"'Bloody hell, I've got a lump coming up under my arm," said another, looking very worried.

"Hang on; didn't that bloke say you got to keep your arm swinging to stop the lump coming up?"

"Come 'ere," said a big bloke grabbing hold of the bumper shaft. They all started to try and take the bumper from one another as one said, "I've got a lump as well."

Looking around the room, Barry could see lots of white faces, all looking very worried.

## Chapter 15

## Moving On

Soon their six weeks of basic training would be finished. They could march in time, turn right or left wheel and about turn without shouting ONE, TWO, THREE, ONE, TWO, THREE in time as they were performing the manoeuvre. They could lay out their kit on their beds and they all thought they were the bee's knees. But no one knew where they were going.

The day came and, having packed their kit, they all were told to get on the back of the trucks. For once the NCOs were very nice to them; that is to say, they were not shouting. The Sappers were told they would be going to Farnborough near Aldershot.

Sitting on the wooden benches either side of the back of the green Bedford trucks with just one corporal sitting at the end next to the tailgate, the Sappers chattered like a load of hens. Having filed on to the train, on which they were the only passengers, they continued to talk about how good they were at marching, bulling their kit and how they were the best ever. Some told jokes, others took the piss out of their mates, and yet others tried to sleep in the racket.

After some hours the train arrived at Farnborough, having not stopped at any stations on the way from Malvern. They were met by a number of NCOs standing on the station platform all looking very smart, their black boots gleaming, belt buckles shining and each tapping their swagger stick against their trousers. They looked into the carriages as they marched up and down the platform, shouting, "All out! Line up in single file!" The Sappers filed out of the station to the waiting trucks and were told to get in, some still chattering.

As the trucks drove out of the station, they continued their chatter. The Corporal, deep in his own thoughts and sitting in the end seat by the open canvas flap which fixed to the tailgate when closed, ignored them. Little did they know what the next fifteen weeks was going to bring!

After a drive of about twenty minutes, the trucks pulled into camp through the gates and past the guardhouse, none of which could be seen by the Sappers from behind the tarpaulin sheets which covered the sides of the trucks. The Sappers were still talking and laughing at silly jokes. Suddenly, the trucks braked hard coming to a stop and throwing all but the NCOs forward on to the man sitting next to them, kit bags flying into a mass of bodies. The NCOs jumped over the tailgates and ran around the side of the trucks. They began to run their swagger sticks down the metal sides of the vehicle making one hell of a racket. "Get the f***k out now! On the double! Line up!" they were all shouting.

Bodies were flying over the tailgate. Some tried to open the gate and one fell on the ground, his kit bag on top of him, right in front of Barry. An NCO saw him and grabbed his kit bag whilst the Sapper got up. He shouted as he threw the bag at him, You f*****g lazy bastard! Get up! Get in line!"

They all fell in and were marched into their wooden billets known as a Spider because of the eight legs. Six billets with the beds, one for the bogs and showers and the other a drying room for wet clothes. All were joined at the entrance via a small hall. They were all sent to their billets and Barry noticed that they had the luxury of central heating with a long radiator at the end of the room which had metal fins and two others down each side. Far better than the old iron coal fire which had looked like an upturned dustbin, and which had sat in the centre of their polished floor at Malvern, thought Barry.

Just inside the room, to one side of the door, were a number of six feet high tin lockers set in an L-shape which, with the two corner walls, made a room with just a gap where a door should be. Barry later discovered this was where Corporal Hann laid down his 'sweet head'. Down each side of the room were a number of green metal beds, mostly single beds, with a dark green metal wardrobe set between them. At the end near the door, almost opposite the opening to Corporal Hann's 'room', were two sets of bunk beds. Barry ended up with a bottom bunk.

"Room conservatory in twenty minutes and get your f*****g kit laid out!" The shouting voice made everyone jump. It would seem, to any member of the public looking in and who had never served in the forces, like animals in the zoo rushing around, laying things out, shouting, climbing over beams.

"Who's got the yard stick?" A stick used to measure the length of the sheets and blankets made up into a pack at head end of the bed.

"Where's the bloody bumper?"

"Who's nicked my best boots?"

"F**k, I've dropped the bloody duster," said a voice from the beam above.

"Stand by your beds!" the shout went out from the doorway. The young sprogs all moved at double time to the side of their beds, each standing ram rod straight with their arms down the sides of their trousers and thumbs in line with the seams.

In marched a Sergeant and two Corporals, the Sergeant carrying a swagger stick. He walked to the back of the room and started to inspect one line. One of the Corporals climbed up on to the roof beams, the other began to inspect the opposite line.

Barry was in the line being inspected by the Sergeant, looking across the room at his opposite number in the other line.

The NCOs were shouting and balling out the Sappers. "What do you call this crap! It's a pile of shit!" Barry heard the boots hit the floor, but he dared not move his head to look.

"It's f*****g filthy up here, Serg," said the Corporal from up on the beams.

"What's this? There's a bloody great heap of dirt in this mug?" said the Sergeant as he almost put the mug up a Sapper's nose. Suddenly, he turned and smashed the bottom of the mug on the end of the radiator leaving a neat hole. *Shit*, thought Barry, *that's going to cost two bob to replace*.

Hearing a sob, Barry slowly turned his eyes, without turning his head, to look at the Sapper facing him in the opposite line. The poor bloke was crying! Suddenly, Barry could see the funny side of the antics and began to grin, realising whatever they do they can't kill you, just go with the flow.

"What are you bloody grinning about?" the Sergeant said as he almost put his stick up Barry's nose. His face was distorted as he stared into Barry's eyes. "Come with me, you little wanker." Barry followed the Sergeant, wondering what was coming next as they entered the toilet area, known as the bogs to all the Sappers.

The Sergeant faced the urinal, a long stainless-steel trough with a high back fixed to the wall. The trough ended with a brass ring with slots to let the urine through after catching the dog ends. He used his stick to pick up the ring and swung it over to Barry.

"Pick that up and polish it until I can see my face in it. Now, double up and get back to billet and finish the cleaning."

"Yes, Sergeant!"

As Barry got back to the room the Sergeant walked in and stood by the door. "Stand to attention!" he bellowed. "This room is in a shit state, you have one hour to clean it up."

The Sergeant and his team marched out. All the Sappers started to flap around, some climbing the beams, others shining their boots and remaking their bed packs. One had made a grab for the bumper and was polishing the floor. Tin locker doors were open, and clothes laid out in neat lines and folded without a crease.

Barry still had to finish his, having spent his time cleaning the brass ring. He rushed out the room to the Sergeant's side room and tapped on the door. "Enter!" bellowed the voice. Barry entered and came to a smart attention.

"I've cleaned this Sergeant," he said as he handed over the ring. The Sergeant took a quick look.

"F*****g filthy, go and clean it again!"

Barry went back to the room and thought, *I am not going to finish cleaning my gear if I spend time doing this ring. Bugger, I'll have to clean my gear.*

One hour later, on the dot, the three NCOs marched into the room. "Stand by your beds!"

When the Sergeant got to Barry he said, "Where's that piss ring, Walker?"

"Here, Sergeant," he said as he handed over the ring.

The Sergeant looked at it and said, "Why couldn't you do it like that in the first place?"

Barry did not say a word, he had never touched it the second time!

Days and nights for the next two weeks were interrupted by football rattles, or a dustbin lid rolled down the centre of the floor, waking up the Sappers at three in the morning to clean the room. During the day, marching on the square or down to the 'Hard', a hard-packed area on the side of a lake, to learn to build Bailey bridges to cross the lake.

Room cleaning settled down with not so many inspections and only during the morning or evening. The weeks ticked on, building a shelter in the form of a five-foot hole in the shape of a W and then covered over. *This was to protect us from an atomic bomb!*

The Sappers were taken to a range to fire their rifles and to strip down a Bren gun and put it back together within a certain time.

One day they were taken to a large pit where they made ring mains and set off plastic explosives. Another day they had a six-mile run in Field Service Marching Order (FSMO). The kit comprised of a tin hat covered in netting, a rifle, two ammunition packs, a large back pack, boots, webbing and lots more. When running, the tin hat would hit the back of the neck and hurt like mad. They were put into teams each under the control of a Corporal who all wanted their team to make the best time.

As the saying goes, time marches on and all the young Sappers were fitter, doing as they were told and being shaped into an Army unit. But they were getting more homesick, not having had any leave.

One early evening when they were all in the billet, Barry approached Corporal Hann.

"Corp, how about letting me go home, this weekend?"

"Don't be daft, you'll go AWOL." (Absent Without Leave)

The weeks wore on and Barry and the others had not had any leave, and some were getting homesick. Those who were married with children could not stop thinking and talking about their sons or daughters.

As Barry did not live far from the camp, he decided to see if he could get leave for thirty-six hours and approached Corporal Hann. "Corporal, any chance I can have a thirty-six?" said Barry looking up at his face. Hann was about six foot three.

"No!"

"Come on, Corporal, I only live in North Kent."

"What do you want to go home for?"

"See my Mum and my mates."

"That's no bloody reason and you might go AWOL!"

"I won't go AWOL, and I'll be back on Sunday." Barry could feel that Hann was weakening. "I can go down to the station at Farnborough and catch a train to Waterloo and cross the platform to catch one to Swanley."

"You know I can't give you a pass. If you get caught, I never gave you permission and you will have to go in uniform. Anyway, how are you going to get past the Guard House?"

"Don't worry, Corporal, I know a way."

"Piss off, I don't want to know. Remember I did not give you permission."

Some of the lads had been listening and as soon as Hann had gone out of the room they turned to Barry.

"You lucky bugger, wish I could go!"

"How are you getting out?"

"There's a hole in the fence just behind the RPs (Regimental Police) jail."

Barry went off in his uniform to Farnborough Station to catch the train to Waterloo and then on to Swanley. He had a great weekend eating, sleeping and boozing. Time flew by and it was soon Sunday afternoon. His mother said, "Do you get much cake in the Army, boy?"

"No, Mum."

"I'll make you up a parcel to take back."

As Barry was leaving a little while later, his Mum gave him a cuddle and pressed a ten-pound note in his hand together with a bag full of goodies.

The journey back to Waterloo was uneventful but as he got off the train, he noticed three pairs of Red Caps (Military Police) walking around the concourse, some of them stopping to check the passes of soldiers. *Shit*, Barry thought, *if they stop me, I'm for the high jump, I'll end up in the glass house* (Military prison).

Feeling very nervous, but trying not to show it, Barry approached the train timetable board to find the time of the next train calling at Farnborough. He stood there studying the timetable just as two Red Caps, who he could see out the corner of his eye, passed him by. He turned, almost shaking, and sat down on a nearby seat where he could still see the train timetable, hoping the train would be early.

Having managed to get to Farnborough without being stopped, he hurried back to the hole in the fence and into the room to be greeted by three voices shouting, "Walker, Corporal Jones wants you, you'd better get to his room at the double!"

"What's he want?"

"Well, he came and did roll call and we put two pillows under your blanket, so he would think you were asleep. But he pulled the blanket off."

"What did he do that for?"

"Because three of us all called out 'Here Sir' but when he shouted out your name…"

"Oh shit! I got this far without trouble and now you lot put me in it! And I brought you back some food."

"Sorry!" they all said simultaneously.

Barry went to Corporal Jones' room and tapped on the door.

"Come in."

Barry entered to see two of the NCOs sitting in the room with mugs of tea in their hands.

"Walker, where the f**k have you been?"

Barry suddenly noticed Corporal Hann sitting on the side of the bed looking sheepish as he looked down, trying not to catch his eye.

"Just home, Corporal."

Having slowly calmed down Jones said, "Get back to your pit, we will deal with this tomorrow, but I will have to report this to the Lieutenant."

When Barry got back to the Spider the lads asked him how he had got on and having told them he would have to wait until tomorrow, he opened up Mum's goody bag. He was suddenly everyone's best friend.

Next day after breakfast they were all lined up and made to double to the camp cinema which turned out to be a wooden hut with double doors at the entrance and a white screen hanging on the back wall inside. They filed in, sat down on the hard metal seats and started to chat.

"What are we going to see?"

"A sex film."

"Do they teach sex in the Army?"

Some of them started to laugh, "Yeah, all those fat birds with big tits, you know the ones you stick your mouth in and blow bubbles."

"Cor, I'm getting a hard on thinking about it," said another rubbing his hand up and down his crutch.

"Shut up, you lot!" came a voice from one of the NCOs as the lights went out.

The film started with naked black men on the screen all of whom had erections, their massive tools poking out. The camera zoomed in on one penis as the voice-over was describing a venereal disease. "As you can see, there are sores on the end of his penis and there is puss coming out." There was an almighty crash and a six-foot-tall Sapper built like a brick shit house fainted, collapsing on to the floor.

"You two, pick that man up and take him outside," a Sergeant's shout rang out.

As the Sapper was being carried out, another voice rang out, "Walker to meet me at the double!" Barry got up from the chair and began to double up towards the voice. Once outside, the Corporal said in a loud voice, "Double to the office," as he ran alongside Barry.

They entered a room in the wooden building, Barry marching in as the Corporal said, "Sapper Walker, Serg."

The Sergeant stood up from behind his desk. He picked up his stick, his face beginning to go slightly red as he worked himself up for the verbal onslaught on Barry. He stood all five feet high as he seemed to go up on tiptoe with his face two inches from Barry. "What bloody stupid excuse have you got for going AWOL?" he said as spittle hit Barry on the face. Barry did not answer at first but tried to look over the Sergeant's head.

The Sergeant was now getting mad. "Why did you go AWOL, you little shit?" he bellowed as he started to hit his leg with the stick, trying to intimidate Barry.

Barry decided he would have to say something. "No reason, Sergeant."

"What did you say?"

"No reason, Sergeant!"

The Sergeant turned and knocked on a door, opened it and marched in closing the door behind him. Standing still at attention, Barry could hear voices. Suddenly, the door opened, and the Sergeant addressed the Corporal, "Bring the Sapper in, Corporal, at the double."

Barry doubled through the doorway in front of the Corporal, stood at attention ramrod straight in front of a desk, glanced at the Officer and gave one of his best salutes. Facing him sitting at the desk the young Officer glanced down at some files on his desk.

"What's the charge, Sergeant?"

"AWOL, Sir."

"Name and number, Sapper?"

"Walker 23575433, Sir."

"What's your excuse?"

"None, Sir."

The Sergeant turned to look at Barry. His face, which Barry could see out the corner of his eye, was bright red. If looks could kill, Barry felt he would by now be suffering a horrible death. *Maybe he has lost face because I did not give him an excuse*, thought Barry.

"Three nights behind the guard; take him away, Sergeant."

Barry was marched up to the Guard House to be given his duties and his name was written on the defaulters' list on a board fixed to the back wall of the Guard House. He was told to report to the cookhouse after he had been on parade. He had to get dressed in his best FSMO and stand behind the Guard on the square. He would then be inspected by the Officer of the Day. The first evening he asked around the room if he could borrow their best webbing to make sure he did not get extra nights behind the guard for having dirty gear.

Having marched on the square, he stood at attention in front of the flag pole and behind the guard, just in time to see out the corner of his eye the Officer and Sergeant marching on to the square.

He marched to the cookhouse, keeping an eye open in case Black Mac was around so that he could dive into the nearest building if he appeared. Black Mac was the worse WO2 in the whole camp who would look at you and find some reason to put you on a charge. Later, whilst still serving, Barry was told by another Sapper that Black Mac was charged with stabbing his wife.

The Sergeant in the cookhouse took him to a small storage room and pointed to a number of sacks. "Here's your knife, over there is a bin; half fill it with water and start peeling the spuds. When you have finished a sack come and find me." *Bloody hell*, thought Barry, *I will never get that lot done before lights out*.

The next evening, having come back from the Hard where the Sappers had been working on building a Bailey bridge on the hard side of a lake, hence the name, they all filed into the Spider completely shattered.

"'Ere, ain't you suppose' to be behind the Guard tonight, Barry?"

"Oh shit, I haven't cleaned my best gear."

"Well, go around and ask to borrow some."

All the others started to help out with their best equipment and Barry began to get dressed as quickly as he could.

"I've got to go or I'll be on another charge," he said as he flew out of the door. He turned around the Spider and walked down the side of the building ready to march onto the square. As he looked in the direction of the Guard, he could see they were all lined up ready for inspection. He glanced to the right and the edge of the square.

*Shit, the Inspecting Officer is just coming on, I'm in trouble if I go on now*, he thought.

Thinking quickly, he ran into the next Spider down the side of the building and flew into the bogs, straight into a cubical and slammed the door.

Barry sat there for some time trying to work out how long the Guard would be before they marched to the guardhouse. He suddenly remembered that his name was on the defaulters' board; he was going to be in massive trouble now!

The days of square bashing, building bridges, digging holes for the latrines (with their straining bars to hold onto whilst having a shit) kept them all busy but Barry only thought of the time when the NCOs would come to get him in the evenings.

Luck was with him, they never did come to find him!

# Chapter 16

# Bored

They had nearly finished their trade training and the postings were on the board. Each Sapper had been given the chance to choose between a posting to the Far East, Near East or home. Barry, who had always wanted to travel, had requested a posting to the Far East but was being sent to West Germany which was considered a home posting. It was a lesson that Barry was quick to learn, the Army always works in reverse! Those Sappers who were married with children, having requested a home posting, would be sent to the Far East and the single chaps would stay in the UK.

"Good, Walker," a shout went out from the doorway as the NCO marched in, "to me at the double."

*What have I done wrong now?* thought Barry.

Good was a slim, fit bloke with dark hair and an Italian look, who looked as if he always needed a shave. Barry was the same height, not quite as slim and with a fairer complexion.

They were marched into the Squadron Office, came to attention and told to wait. Barry was beginning to think that he was going to be on a charge for not finishing his three nights behind the guard.

"Good, follow me," said the NCO.

Barry wondered what Good had done wrong as he took a glance around the room without moving his head. Any movement from his ram rod straight position would draw the attention of the NCOs who were shuffling papers as they sat at their desks, and he did not want to be on another charge.

The green (it seemed to Barry that everything in the Army was painted green) door opened and Good marched through with a lost look on his face.

It was Barry's turn and he too marched through the green door, came to attention and did one of his best salutes to the Captain and the Major who were sitting behind a desk, each with a file in front of them.

Questions, questions and more questions.

"That's all, take him out."

Barry looked for Good as soon as he got back to the Spider. "What was that all about, Good?"

"Beats me, but we'll soon find out!"

Training was coming to an end with only a few weeks to go until the passing out parade when all the parents would be invited to watch the parade. But Barry would not be marching. He had an arm in a sling due to boils which he must have contracted from dirty water. However, he still had to clean and polish his kit and prepare his uniform to wear on the day. But as time went on the NCOs eased back on the inspections until the day before the big parade.

Barry had at last been given his posting, not the Far East, not the Middle East, not Germany but a home posting as Batman to the two officers who interviewed him and the other Sapper.

Barry thought, *I wonder why they chose me?* Then it dawned on him. The other chap was good looking, *not an ugly bugger like me*. They were worried about their wives getting up to no good!

Barry moved his kit from the Spider on the training side of the camp square to the camp staff Spider and packed his kit away. Now that he was a member of staff he had a number of benefits, the most important of which, he discovered, was that he was not on the training camp staff but attached to HQ as his officers were based there. He used a bike to get to the officers' houses; he did not have to go on parade every day and he obtained a late breakfast pass. Once he had finished his duties – cleaning the officers' belts, shoes, pressing uniforms and a little cleaning in the house and garden – he was free to leave to go back to camp.

Being in the staff Spider, in a room of about ten Sappers, he soon made friends; some were from the armoury and one from the Regimental Police. They were a mixed bunch in the billet and Barry's pit was near the door. Towards the end of the room four Sappers, two each side, would make the most noise after they came back from a drinking session in Aldershot. They would play who could make the most farts, sometimes getting into the upper twenties.

"'Ere, Fred, bend over and stick your bare arse up," said one as he took a box of matches out of his pocket. Just as Fred farted, he lit a match and blue flames shot out of his arse! The four cheered. "Come on, do it again," they roared.

"How many farts is that?"

"Twenty-seven, I reckon he'll shit himself on number twenty-eight!"

On the other side of the room from Barry was a well-built chap who loved to parade in the nude, showing off his big dick putting the rest of the normal people in the shade. His nickname was Big Dick.

Barry had a great advantage over his fellow Sappers. He was not on the camp's strength and his ration book was kept in Aldershot. No camp duties, no parades and no guard duties. He would rise with the rest of them, do his ablutions, make his bed and slowly stroll down to the cookhouse and chat to the NCO as he went behind to the kitchen to cook his own breakfast.

Barry soon settled in, cleaning, gardening, and even babysitting which he liked to do as there was always a meal and the television.

Having settled down to his new work day, Barry started to get bored with the same old things and while on a 48-

hour pass, he decided to bring his A35 van back to camp. He did not realise how popular he would be! As soon as word got around that he had his van in the car park the requests started.

"Run us up to the 'Swinging Tit'," (the Crown and Cushion Pub, so named after a previous landlady with big swinging breasts) asked George, "and I'll buy you a pint."

This was on Monday when he had money in his pocket; by Wednesday most of the Sappers were broke. Thursdays were pay days and as soon as the pub was open and work for the day finished, they all made a beeline to a pub in Aldershot. But the three friends always went to the more upmarket pub.

George and Barry had a system. They would save some of their pay by placing money, with which to buy their beer, on the optics until next pay day.

Like most pubs and groups, many were given nicknames and one such was Curly, a tall, bald, quiet man, with whom George, John and Barry became friends over time.

It was Wednesday and George and Barry sat leaning on the bar looking miserable and not saying a word.

"What's wrong with you two? Why did I ask, I know you've got no money for your beer," said Curly as he put his hand in his pocket to buy them a beer.

"Thanks, Curly," they said in unison and smiling, having cheered up, "we'll buy you one when we get our pay."

Billeted with Barry was a member of the Regimental Police, their gaol being just to the back of the camp and up on a rise.

"'Ere, Barry, they are cutting pit poles near the Hard," said Fred.

"So what, you want me to go and pick them up?"

"No, you twat, we could cut them up for logs and flog them."

"Let's go and have a look tonight before it gets dark."

After supper, Fred and Barry made their way around the back of the Spiders towards the lake, to an area cleared of trees. It was covered in small bushes with pit poles or logs scattered in amongst them.

Barry looked at the logs, "They're fine but how are we going to cut them up and where do we get some sacks?"

"We can pinch some of the sacks they use for sand bags, and I can borrow a chain saw."

"OK, but now I've got to find some customers," said Barry.

Barry looked around, working out the best way to bring his van in to load up. Scattered around were small Christmas trees, some blocking the way. *Just a minute*, thought Barry, *I could flog those to the Officers*. For a while the two of them ran the little business but then a new venture took its place.

The camp had an internal radio system with speakers in each billet. These were used to send messages and to call Sappers, and in the evening to try and keep the sprogs happy whilst they were cleaning their kit. They would play records and sometimes have a quiz programme.

Barry could not remember how he was approached, but he found himself presenting a Traditional Jazz programme with guests reviewing the music. At times the show would become a bit of a comedy with the participants falling about with laughter which, he was told, cheered up the sprogs.

Being a training camp, the Sappers were there for nine weeks of trade training after having completed their six weeks basic training. Some had not been home in those fifteen weeks and others had only forty-eight hour passes hence, being male lads between the ages of 21 and 25, they were full of testosterone and wanted female company, in spite of the bromide they put in the tea.

"Mike," said Barry addressing the technical chap, "I've an idea, can you rig up some sort of way that I can travel around the spiders and interview some of the Sappers?"

"Yeah, I can fix up something. But what do you want to do that for, it won't be very interesting."

"It will, if I take a bird with me."

"You do that, and you'll be on a charge!"

"Only if they find out! How many of the Officers listen to our crap; all the young ones will be in the mess pissing it up and the NCOs will be in their mess doing the same or at home with their families."

"OK, I'll help."

It only remained for Barry to find a "nice young lady" to agree to go into a billet full of randy blokes after he had smuggled her into the camp. It so happened that he was teaching a girl to drive in his A35 van and after a lot of chat he persuaded her to give it a try.

"Who's the girl you are going to bring?" said Mike.

"A girl who nearly smashed my van up."

"What!"

"She tried to kiss the arse of a lorry with the green bonnet of my van and now she walks with a limp."

"Why?"

"I stamped on her brake foot to stop her."

The day came when Julie was due to meet the Sappers and thirty minutes before they were due to be on the radio Barry arrived at camp with Julie in the back of his van. The Guards knew Barry and his little van and just waved him through. Having parked out of sight of the Guard House, he rushed Julie into the radio studios, praying she had not been seen as the camp was completely male only.

Barry introduced Mike to Julie.

"Cor, you look smashing! The sprogs will go mad."

Julie was wearing a green summer dress which hugged her slim waist over two or three petticoats which came down to just below her knees. Her blond hair would swing in time to the swing of her hips as she walked. The top of her dress had two string straps showing off her silky, slightly tanned skin. Her voice was low pitched and slightly sexy, the sound of which should get the attention of the sappers over the radio.

"Let's get this show on the road," said Barry as he turned to Mike, who could not keep his eyes off Julie. "Let's try the first Spider. I'll go in first and get their attention; you wait for me to call you in."

As soon as the men caught sight of Julie, they were almost falling over each other to get near to her. Barry was doing his best to keep the mic in front of each speaker as they were all trying to flirt with her. Julie was loving it! There were going to be many wet dreams tonight.

# Chapter 17

# Captured

Barry and George were enjoying a pint in the Swinging Tit early one summer evening.

"As you've got the van here, Barry, can you run us over to the Hard, I've issued out rifles and other gear to the TA for their exercise."

"What! Live ammo for those Territorial Army wallahs, they'll kill themselves."

"Don't be daft, they're blank's. I just want to check they haven't damaged the kit otherwise I'll be for it."

Barry and George set off down an undulating track through the woods which surrounded a hard landing area where Bailey bridges were built, and landing craft were kept. The van bounced about over the pot holes and George, being over six foot tall, kept hitting his head on the roof of the van.

"Slow down, you idiot, we're not going to a fire!" said George as they hit another pot hole.

Suddenly there was an almighty BANG quickly followed by another on the other side of the rear body of Barry's van.

"Christ, what the f***?"

"You're captured!" came a voice followed by another as two guys in uniform grabbed the doors each side, carrying pick up handles as they held on.

"Get off my van!" yelled Barry.

"Just follow the track, Sir!"

"I'm not going anywhere until I know what's going on."

George butted in, "Just do as they say; we can sort it out later."

With the van bouncing over the pot holes and the two soldiers hanging on for dear life, Barry attempted to shake them off but to no avail. Eventually they arrived in a dip in the track surrounded by trees after having passed through a guard post of four more soldiers wearing yellow arm bands. Looking ahead they could see a number of camouflaged trucks set out in a clearing.

"Stop here and don't get out."

"Where's the C.O., Serg?" said one of the men to a passing Sergeant.

"In Aldershot."

"Any other Officers about?"

"No, they're all up at the camp mess."

"What do I do with these prisoners?"

"Take them to the booze wagon until one of the Officers gets back."

Barry and George were taken across the clearing to a camouflaged Bedford lorry parked under trees. Two soldiers were standing at the back of the lorry which had its canvas top rolled up and the bottom tailgate folded down. The soldiers both had pint glasses full of beer. They were looking across at Barry and George, who were in civvies, wondering who the hell they were and whether they should hide their beer.

The chap who had captured them turned and said, "What will you have, bitter?"

"Make mine a mild," said George. "What's with the yellow arm bands?"

"Well, the blue bands are the enemy, and you must be spies."

"Come on, I'm the Armourer and this is my driver," said George pointing to Barry.

Well, that was the start of another session. The TA got the Armourer and Barry pissed and the Officers never did turn up. Barry managed to drive his van through the trees into the back of the camp, park up and fall into his pit.

John, who had a pit at the end of the billet, approached Barry late one afternoon. "Barry, any chance I could borrow your van?"

"What for?"

"Well, I've got this date and I want to take her out."

"Where are you going to take her?"

John, who was just a little shorter than Barry with fair hair, almost blond, and what might be called a boyish look, pouted and said in a slightly embarrassed way, "I'm hoping to get my end away!"

"What, in the back of my van? What have you got to lie on?"

"I'll take my bedding."

Barry, looking a bit pensive, said, "When do you want to borrow the van?"

"Tonight."

"Impossible, I'm babysitting for Captain Winkel, and I need the van."

"That's not a problem; you can use my motorbike and side car."

"But I don't have a licence to ride a bike."

"Bloody hell, that's not a problem! It's only down the road and there are no cops about."

"OK then, but clean the van out; I don't want a load of used condoms floating about in the back and stinking it out!"

John went off to meet his date after the swap of keys and a quick run through for Barry on the controls on the motorbike. It was then that Barry realised it had a sidecar.

The kids were in bed when Barry arrived at Captain Winkel's, and he spent the evening watching the TV and dozing. He heard the front door open at about midnight.

"Everything alright, Walker?"

"Yes, Sir."

"Off you go then and thank you."

It was pitch black outside as Barry tried to start the bike. After three or four tries the bike started and he drove down to the lane to the Camp, missed the turning and ended up on the grass bank twisted in the mud.

"Shit! And bugger! I forgot to steer it instead of leaning around the corner," Barry said to himself.

Puffing and panting, he managed to pull the bike out and set about trying to start the 'bloody thing'. Having spent nearly half an hour trying he gave up and started to push at the same time as trying to steer. It was late and dark as he pushed the bike along the lane like a drunken Sapper, stopping every few yards to rest. "Here I am knackered pushing this bloody beast whilst he's having it away in the back of my van!"

The two years National Service was coming to an end for some of Barry's friends who were getting demob happy. John, who was nearly three years older than Barry and who had to finish his training in civvy street as a Ship's Architect, invited Barry and George to stay at his home near Bournemouth for the weekend. They all set off in Barry's van after work on a Friday afternoon. Barry, from a working-class background, had never stayed in someone else's house and he was a little apprehensive not knowing what to expect.

John was giving directions as they reached Bournemouth, and it soon became clear that his family lived in Poole in a large white house with a long back garden reaching down to the water. Looking out into the bay Barry could see a number of yachts swing on their anchors.

"Which one is yours, John?" said Barry in a jokey way.

"That large white one at anchor."

"What, it belongs to you?"

"No, you wally, it's my Dad's."

Being used to Army grub, the three of them were starting to feel hungry and Barry was just about to ask John's mother for something to eat when John's father came in.

"Shall we go to the Dolphin for dinner?" he said looking at John.

"That will be great," said John.

"We will get changed," he shouted as he ran up the stairs pushing Barry and George in front of him.

At the end of the evening when George and Barry were standing outside of the Dolphin, Barry said to George, "As I have never been to a restaurant before, how did I do?"

"Well, you did OK, watching others and copying, but you were holding your steak knife upside down!"

The three lads decided to go into Bournemouth on Saturday to a dance hall and see if they could pick up some girls after a few beers. George who was six feet three, Barry around five ten, and John five nine, were standing near the dance floor watching the girls and the odd bloke dancing. The girls were in their pretty dresses of pink, pale blue and red with four or five petticoats under them. With belts setting off their slim waists, most of them had ponytails swinging as they danced.

"I fancy that one in the blue dress," commented George.

"Cor, so do I," said Barry.

"Bit tall for you, Barry, and you can't dance."

"OK, I'll bet you ten bob I can pick her up and have a dance with her?"

George and John cried out in unison, "You're on!"

Barry, sliding across the floor came up to the girl and said, "Fancy a dance?"

"All right then."

Doing his best not to tread on the girl's toes and as he looked up into her eyes, Barry said "You look lovely, fancy going to the pictures tomorrow?"

"OK."

They met outside the cinema and Barry splashed out on the most expensive seats so they could sit at the back. They cuddled up and kissed during the slow bit is the picture, both feeling sensuous and sometimes getting very excited. The music playing in the background was 'A Summer Place'.

It was a warm, summer evening, so they went for a walk on the sandy beach. She was two inches taller than Barry. They fondled and kissed as she leant against a wall when suddenly she said, "Barry, what do you do?"

Thinking fast, Barry thought, *I can't tell her I'm still in the Army, she may think I'm after a one-night stand and clear off.* "Well, I'm down here on a construction job, I'm an engineer," he said.

Every time Barry heard that music he thought of that evening.

Later Back at the camp, on checking the chart stuck on the inside door of his locker, Barry could see he had only just over six weeks before his demob. He asked for two weeks' leave to go home to see if he could earn some money and make sure he had a job to go back to at J & E Hall.

It was early October, and the apples were about to be picked. From the back door of his parents' house, he looked down the long garden over the fences and the alley to the apple trees laden with fruit. The trees were set in the grounds of an industrial laundry which served a number of hospitals in Kent. Barry's Dad worked there as the pipe and maintenance fitter. Later when his Dad came home, he asked if he had some sacks and if he could pick as many apples as he could carry.

Two days later Barry took three sack loads to a shop in Dartford and, having chatted to the owner, they agreed a price. Pocketing the money, he got talking to him about a job.

"Sorry, but I don't need any extra help," said the shop owner. "I know the Co-op bakery is always looking for people to work on their night shift."

The next night Barry was on the bread line!

As Barry walked into the building the heat hit him, like walking into an oven, which in fact it was, making him catch his breath.

Looking around he thought, *This must be something like a Dickens sweat shop.* The men were all in their vests, skins gleaming with sweat in the overhead lights. Around their middle they had bits of sacking, as aprons, tied with string; most of them were white with flour. Three men were working at a table positioned under a stainless-steel tube hanging down from the ceiling from which dough was slowly emerging. They would, it seemed, grab a handful in turn and start to knead it into a lattice shaped like a pigtail. These were then taken to the oven to be cooked.

To the right of the men was a conveyor with tins, four in a row horizontally, coming down from the floor above. There were three more rows that Barry could see, and the conveyor was moving quite fast. Working on this section were two other chaps who were each wearing bits of sacking on their hands like gloves. They were taking the tins off the conveyor whilst it was still moving and banging the tins on the edge of the machine. The loaves fell on to another conveyor taking the bread away. The sacking on their hands was to protect them from the heat. The smell of hot bread seemed to float around the building. Barry was put on the conveyor to empty the bread tins and was told there were breaks every two hours to drink water.

This was Barry's last leave before he left the Army.

## CIVVY STREET

# Chapter 18

# Civvy Street

Barry was back in civvy street after his two years in the Royal Engineers, working nights in his old job. He would clock in at seven in the evening and have a break for some tea and sandwiches from one till two am and finish work at seven in the morning.

Civilian life was not as he remembered. He missed his old friends, the gang, the band, going out to dance halls, meeting girls and the odd pub crawl. All his old friends had flown the nest to the four corners. Some were now married; others had long-term girl friends or new jobs. He missed his mates from the Army, his two best friends, one currently working in Troon in Scotland and the other in Manchester.

In the afternoons and at weekends he was at a loose end, driving around in his almost new car, a Singer, looking for some interesting places to go in the hope of finding a girl to befriend.

During the night, the machine shop only had half the number of people working as on the day shift. There was always one labourer clearing up the floor during the night and Barry would sometimes chat to him as he was sweeping around his machine. They became friendly and one night he asked Barry if he would like to come to his daughter's evening reception at her wedding.

Having accepted, Barry turned up at the hall to the sound of music. Entering he looked around for someone he might know, but to no avail, and decided to get something to eat from the table at the back.

The small group of three musicians on drums and two guitars were trying to play some of the hits of the 50s.

Having finished his food, he took his plate through to the kitchen which was through a doorway at the side of the stage and stood leaning against the door frame listening to the band.

"Hello," said a young girl standing in front of him, looking up all googly eyed.

He noticed she had freckles and was wearing a red frock with black dots which flared out from her slim waist down, with a number of white petticoats underneath, looking just like a pretty doll. *I think she is trying to chat me up,* thought Barry.

"Hello, what's your name?" said Barry.

"Mavis, what are you doing here?" she asked. "I haven't seen you around before."

"I was invited by the bride's father."

They tried to talk over the sound of the band and Barry started to move away. Mavis was approached by another girl, and they started talking, leaving Barry to eye up the talent to see if he could get a date.

Finding few girls who were not dancing, he got into conversation with two fellows and a tubby girl who were talking about cars. "Whose car is that Singer in the car park?" There were only two cars parked there.

"Mine," said Barry. The conversation went on for a while, but Barry was getting bored. Turning his head he spotted a gorgeous looking girl. He approached her and started to chat her up, mentioning his car.

"Come and have a look and I'll take you for a drive."

"OK."

Barry took her for a drive through the streets of Dartford, which did not take long as there were few cars around in 1960, and up on to the Heath where he stopped. He tried to chat her up whilst trying to put his arms around her; she was so pretty with her slim waist and her blue and white dress. All to no avail, all she wanted was a ride in his car!

When he got back to the wedding reception, who should try to chat him up but the tubby girl who told him she lived in a pub and could he give her a lift. "What, now?" said Barry.

"Yes please," she said with a sickly smile, "it's only just down the road."

Barry relented and took her home hoping to get a free drink. The pub turned out to be the Bull Hotel and she got out of the car in a rush. "Will I see you again?"

"I'll call you," said Barry as he drove away.

Fed up, Barry headed back and decided to go to the pub across from the hall as there was no booze at the wedding. He walked into the bar and who should be there but Mavis, sitting on some chap's lap!

"What are you doing in here? You're too young to be in a pub drinking."

"No, I am not," said Mavis indignantly and picked up her bag and started to rummage inside. "There, look at the date," she said handing over her birth certificate. She was twenty-one but looked sixteen.

About a week later Barry was working on his machine during the night shift when the labourer came up to him and handed him a slip of paper. On it was a telephone number with 'Please phone me. Mavis'.

That was it! Barry was hooked, and on the re-bound from the Army. They were married fifteen months later.

The wedding was fast approaching, all too soon, and Mavis, who was working at Champion and Waterman Estate Agents and Auctioneers who also ran Dartford cattle market, had managed to rent a two up and two down old property with an outside toilet. The toilet did not have any lights and was in a very sorry state. They set about cleaning the place up and decorating, ready to move in after the honeymoon. Barry found a cheap sink unit to replace the old deep stone sink which was on a wooden frame and fixed to the wall. Having measured ready to fit, he started to pull the old sink out and to pull the frame away from the wall. CRASH! Down came part of the wall. "Bloody hell," said Barry coughing from the dust as he was kneeing in front of the wall.

"Mavis, come and look at this."

"What? I'm not getting down on that dirty floor."

"Look, I can see into next door!"

Some weeks later, having finished the decorating inside and hung up the tin bath in the kitchen, they started on the outside. Barry had borrowed a tall ladder and started to paint the side wall and Mavis decided to help by painting along the bottom of the wall. After a while, Barry came down the ladder to get some more paint and bumped into some monster from the deep, Mavis, covered in paint from top to toe.

"You stupid woman, you should not have been under my ladder whilst I was painting!"

The big day came and Barry, his brother Richard and Russ, an Architect friend from his Army days, agreed before going to the Church, to have *just* one or two jars at the pub situated near the Church, a street away.

Being late, and some many pints later, Barry was frog marched – his brother holding one arm, Russ holding the other and his feet hardly touching the ground – to the Church arriving just in time.

Sometime later at the reception as they were cutting the cake, with the knife upside down, Mavis said to Barry, "If you had not turned up when you did, Dad said he was going back home. He had driven around the block three times!"

The wedding breakfast for sixty-seven people, including drinks, cost ninety-four pounds, four shillings and seven pence (£94.23) and took place in the Royal Victoria and Bull Hotel, Dartford, a Dickensian coaching inn. At the centre front of the building there were two large doors as high as a London bus. The doors were painted black and opened into a large internal courtyard.

At the back of the building was a similar opening for the coach and horses to move into the yard to the stables after the passengers had alighted. At the first-floor level on each side of the courtyard was a walkway running from the front to the back of the building. The walkway, servicing the bedrooms, was held up by decorated wooden poles fixed to the roof with yellow fencing between the poles so that guests could stand and look at the activity below. Hanging at intervals from the walkway were leather buckets filled with sand or water for use in case of fire.

After the meal, which lasted some time, a small reception was held at Mavis's mother's house where the bride and groom could change to leave to go on their honeymoon in Torquay.

"Shall we stop on the way, this confetti is making me itch," said Barry, pulling some out from the back of his neck as he drove one handed.

Mavis, who was wearing a grey and white suit with dusty pink shoes said, "We could stop at that big pub the other side of Westerham."

Stopping, they both ran into the pub's toilets and, in the hope that no one would come in, took most of their clothes off and shook them.

They stayed at a large, terraced house in Torquay having booked half board. Every morning Barry would ask for more bread, till by the end of the week he was eating half a loaf! On the Wednesday Mavis said, "Can you ask the lady if I can have a bath?" The bedrooms only had wash basins and the only bathroom was down the hall.

On the day they were leaving, as Barry was finishing the 'The Rise and Fall of the Roman Empire' while waiting for Mavis (at the time he did not realise he would be waiting for the rest of his life!) the lovely lady said, "Until Wednesday when you asked me if your wife could have a bath, I did not know you were a honeymoon couple."

After breakfast one morning, Barry decided to go out to some of the villages he used to visit with the gang before he went into the Army. As it was a sunny day, he would not be able to sleep before he started night work.

By around midday, he began to feel peckish and called in one of the pubs he used to visit in Yalding. After a few pints while eating cheese and pickle and chatting to the locals, he made his way home.

That evening, while working at his machine, he became sleepy and decided to take a break. Switching off the machine, he made his way over to the Tool Room looking around to see if the Foreman was anywhere in sight. Not seeing him, Barry found a bench with some sacks under the bench top. He curled down and was instantly asleep.

Sometime later, he was awoken by someone shaking his arm and upsetting his dream of chasing a semi-nude girl. Half awake, he realised he was holding his erect penis.

"What?" still half asleep and groaning and trying to shake off the hand.

"Wake up, what are you doing?"

As if it wasn't obvious, Barry thought.

"How long have you been under here asleep?" said the Foreman.

Barry, still slightly sluggish, said, "Bugger it, I'm off."

"What do you mean? You don't have to resign."

"I've had enough of this night work, I'm leaving."

After leaving J & E Hall, Barry's first job was at a small firm in east Dartford who were sub-contractors to larger companies obtaining work for machine parts. He soon made friends with the other employees: Sid, who worked the machine behind him, and Ian, a young apprentice, to name two.

One day the works Manager, called Barry up to his small office. "Barry, I'm sorry but the firm is going through a rough patch and as you were the last one in, I will have to let you go."

Barry soon found a new job in Crayford in a much more modern factory where instead of wearing blue overalls he was issued with a white coat.

Some months later he was having a chat to the firm's Inspector who checked the machine parts made by the employees. He was younger than Barry and they talked about setting up a business together. Little did he know this was the beginning of something BIG!

They needed machines and somewhere to work and one day Barry found an advertisement in one of the local papers: 'Garage to rent'. It was next door to Charlton Athletic Football Club's ground, some few miles away. Barry agreed a price for the rent and started to look for used machines.

A few weeks later, Joe, the Inspector, and Barry had set up a bench drill, a small lathe and a welding set. At lunchtime every work day he would tour around the various companies in the nearby towns trying to obtain work.

Barry had no idea how to price for the work or the difference between an invoice and a statement. He did not know how to set out a quotation but over the weeks and months he soon learned. The biggest problem he found was working out how long it would take to make a machine part and what to charge.

He picked up a few small orders, but all the customers wanted them urgently. Barry started work at the factory at 7.30am each weekday and could be seen each lunchtime in his little van delivering the finished parts he had completed the night before. He was now working in the garage till 2.00am every day and all-day Saturday and Sunday while still holding down his day job. His small firm started to become known.

When Barry arrived home, he would enter by the back door and shout out, "I'm home!" One day, looking into the front room and finding no one there and turning past the white painted wood wall on which hung the tin bath, he walked up the stairs to find Mavis in bed, sobbing her eyes out.

"Why can't you just have one job?" she said between sobs.

"I won't have to work so many hours when it gets going, I'll be able to employ someone."

Mavis had two brothers, Norman and Ralph. They had a building firm, and their workshop and yard were at the rear of their parents' house. Barry and Mavis would sometimes have dinner at the house and on one occasion Norman came in while they were eating.

"You know that old wooden shed behind our workshop, where we keep old paint tin," said Norman.

"Yes."

"Would you like to rent it for your workshop for ten shillings per week?"

"Has it got a strong concrete floor?"

"Yes."

Barry moved the machines in some weeks later and started work in the evenings, saving almost an hour's travelling time. His partner worked in the evenings but would not always turn up. Barry was not good at welding and on a rare night that he left early, his partner was due to weld some machine guards needed urgently.

Next day the guards were due to be delivered and Barry went to collect them at 6am before going to work. They were not finished!

Barry's mother-in-law was in the kitchen which overlooked the drive to the workshop, so he called in to see her and ask if she saw him go. "He left just after you last night."

That was the end of the partnership!

Mavis was working at Radio Rentals in Plumsted, South London. At that time, their main business was to rent out TVs. She would leave home to go to work after Barry had left and returned in time to start preparing their evening meal before Barry arrived home. It was wintertime and for the last week or two London's air quality had been getting worse. With no wind, the mist from the River Thames was swirling across the capital joining all the smoke from thousands of fires emitted from homes and offices. The 'pea souper' of a smog, as the locals called it, was just like something from a black and white Dickensian film. A thick, smelly, dirty grey smog with yellow halos forming around the street lights as it got dark. People, some wearing scarves over mouths, could hardly see more than a yard in front as they tried to find their way. Buses and cars moved more slowly than pedestrians.

It was one of those days when Mavis left her work around midday to go home early. After waiting at a bus stop for over half an hour, no buses arrived, so she decided to walk home from Plumsted to Dartford.

It was not long before the bad air started to affect Mavis's lungs; she found it was getting more difficult to breathe and she started to cough. People were walking in front of buses with cars followed by cars. Mavis could hear, but not see, others coughing in the smog. On arriving home at 6.30pm she changed her clothes which were covered in dark brown and black smuts and started to prepare the evening meal. Fifteen minutes later she was as sick as a dog with pain in her back, coughing up muck and feeling tight in her chest!

# Chapter 19

# A New Beginning

Barry had formed the firm into a limited company called White House Precision Engineers (Dartford) Limited. He was beginning to get more orders but was finding it almost impossible to keep up (he was still working seven days a week till late in the evening) and deliver on time, so he decided to take on an employee. He remembered old Sid, who was in his sixties, from the firm he used to work, and Barry parked outside the factory until Sid came out at clocking off time.

Sid started work for Barry two weeks later. He was on his own while Barry carried on working at the factory in Crayford, popping in daily to give Sid his instructions.

They were now getting so busy that Barry would machine parts for his own firm's customers when at his day job, hoping that the foreman did not notice! As time went on, inevitably the foreman did find out and Barry had to stop or hand his notice in. He was faced with a problem: stay, find another job or work in his own firm.

Barry now had two people working for him and the shed had expanded with a tarpaulin fixed over the entrance under which a welder worked. He wanted a job which gave him more time to make deliveries and obtain even more work.

Barry was intrigued by an advertisement in the local paper – *Sales persons needed to introduce Encyclopaedia Britannica* – and decided to apply. He got the job: commission only, no salary and you had to have a car to visit potential customers to show them samples and obtain orders. First, however, you had to get appointments by telephone. In the office where he worked there were banks of phones with screens dividing each phone point. Blocks of names with addresses and telephone numbers, at the cost of one penny per name, had to be purchased.

Where possible, Barry would try to target families so they would buy the books for their children to help with their education. Barry would first show the parents the pretty pictures in the books. He would then offer to throw in a free bookcase to match their furniture and even offered another set of children's books as an incentive to buy.

Barry would spend an hour or two most mornings on the telephone arranging evening appointments and the rest of the day working on a machine.

He only ever sold one set of books!

As a result of Barry's lack of a decent education and the fact he could not spell, the engineering paperwork, invoices, statements and accounts were in a complete muddle. He was starting to get "Red Letter" demands and occasional threatening letters.

Arriving home early one Sunday afternoon as Mavis was ironing in the front room of their two up two down house (the ironing board took up most of the room) this was brought home to him. Barry went to open a small cupboard and as he pulled the handle, masses of paper fell out all over the floor. The scattered papers were invoices, statements and letters demanding payment in red. Mavis went bonkers!!!

"Look at the mess," she said picking up some of the letters. "What's this? It looks like they are going to take us to court," she cried with a worried look on her face.

"Don't worry, I'll sort it. I'm just waiting for some money to come in; some of the customers have not paid me for over four months."

"Well, you had better chase them!"

Having finished phoning for appointments one day, he started talking to the chap in the next cubical about how he earned a living as he had not sold any encyclopaedias.

"I'm an accountant. I have a few clients."

"Why are you doing this then?"

"I was bored and wanted a change."

"Would you be interested in taking on a small engineering company?"

His name was Dormer Anderson and Barry proceeded to tell him about his own company.

Having expanded the company and increased the number of machines and employees, they were running out of room. The small factory, which had formerly been a paint shed, was behind the workshop belonging to Pearson and Sons (Builders). Their yard was nearly a quarter of an acre and had plenty of room to expand with more buildings.

Barry felt it was time to concentrate on his business, pay himself a little more and try to expand further. One day on his way to see a client to try and obtain some more orders, he drove past a small factory which was being demolished. Calling in, he noticed that the building had been a steel frame surrounded by brickwork of about 5,000 sq. ft. Chatting to the man on site, Barry obtained the telephone number of the owner.

Having agreed a price for the steel frame he now had to persuade Norman Pearson, Mavis's brother, to build him a new factory using the metal framework. However, that presented another problem. They would have to find somewhere for the sheet metal work to be carried out as there was no way that this type of work could be conducted in the new factory alongside the other machines.

A stroke of luck! An old Territorial Army (TA) Centre became available alongside Northfleet Football ground. What was to become the factory was a very large, high building with three large sliding doors down one side. The building had been used to store large Army lorries and cranes.

Barry had a discussion with his accountant, Dormer Anderson, and they decided to form another company, White House Fabrication Limited, with Dormer taking 50% of the shares and 5% of the shares in the precision company.

Now that the new building was finished, Barry was spending most of his time obtaining orders, quoting and trying to manage both works. He soon needed help.

# Chapter 20

### Staff Problems

One day there was a tap on Barry's office door at the Dartford factory. "Come in."

"There's a bloke here to see you, Gov."

"I'll come out, thanks."

On opening the door, Barry found a man of medium height wearing a grey suit and tie.

"Barry?"

"Yes," he said in a not too friendly voice as the man, who Barry did not know, was addressing him by his first name.

"My name is Kennedy, I'm Ian's father. Can I speak to you about Ian?"

"Ian, why? Yes, come in. Now, what's the problem?"

"Ian's got the sack, and he hasn't finished his apprenticeship."

"How come; what's he done to warrant getting the sack?"

"He's been mucking about, but I don't believe that's the real reason. I think the firm is going through a difficult time, as they have already sacked another man."

"So, what do you want me to do?"

"Can he finish his apprenticeship with you? He's got two more of his five years to finish."

"OK, tell him to come and see me."

Ian completed his apprenticeship and turned out to be an excellent employee, so much so that within eighteen months of finishing his apprenticeship he was promoted to foreman.

During the times of expansion, the firm was always short of capstan operators. It was during one of these periods that a chap came for an interview. He turned out to be a very quiet, muscular, jet black man and Barry gave him the job.

Some minutes after he left, having been given a starting date of the following Monday, Sid, the firms oldest employee, knocked on the office door.

"Barry, that black chap, you know that if you take him on you are going to have trouble!"

Barry, who had never been colour prejudiced, started to lose it. He hated it when people, who in most cases had never met or spoken to a coloured person, seemed to immediately dislike them. "DON'T you ever say to me who I can or cannot employ! I don't care if they are white, black, yellow or sky blue pink, as long as they can do the job!"

Jo, the new chap, started on the following Monday and for the first two weeks arrived on time and worked well. However, Barry noticed that he did not sit with the other machinists during break times but sat alone.

As weeks went by Jo began to arrive later and later for work. He was told time and again to improve his time keeping. He did not improve.

By now Barry's brother Dick was the works manager at Northfleet and three of them – Ian, Dick and Barry – were having a meeting in his office. Barry had told Jo that he was to leave at the end of the day and to pick up his money as he left.

CRASH! The office door suddenly flew open. Jo came flying in brandishing a large spanner and shouting as he flew at Barry. All hell let loose as Dick and Ian quickly got up as the chairs fell across the floor. They made a grab for Jo's arms. There was one hell of a struggle, and it took the two of them to get him out of the office and factory, with the machinist stopping to look, while Barry phoned the Police. The Police arrived in minutes and held Jo while Barry picked up his things and made up his money. Jo was never seen again, and the consensus was that he had a chip on his shoulder about white workers.

# Chapter 21

# Bank of England

Among the company's clients were many well-known names including Barclays Bank. Barry's contact was an architect who worked for the bank designing and altering bank premises. One of the contracts was at a large building in Lower Thames Street, London. Barry's firm had to supply and fit large cabinets on rails to run along the floor of the basement. After some weeks of making and fitting they finished the job. Two or three days later, Barry was in his office trying to catch up with his paperwork when the phone rang.

"Barry, I'm going to be in the shit, I need your help!" It was the architect from Barclays.

"What's up?"

"I have forgotten to ask you to make a free-standing cabinet, can you make me one?"

"How soon do you want it, what size?"

"Well, I want it yesterday and I don't know what size it is. It's to take the largest physical size of bank note in circulation and never mind the cost, just make it!"

"How can we make it if we don't know the size?"

"The only thing I can suggest is to ask the Bank of England."

"Leave it with me, I'll see what I can do."

Over the telephone Barry was grilled by a man from the Bank of England. "Who are you?"

Barry gave details of himself and the company.

"Why do you want to know? Who is it for?" He then said someone would come back to Barry.

Two more phone calls later and after many more questions, Barry was at last given the size, 10 by 8 inches.

He then had to go back to the architect for him to obtain an estimate of how many currency notes the Bank would normally store.

The cabinet was made overnight with three of the staff working all night.

# Chapter 22

# New Home, New Problems

Mavis's two brothers were building thirty-five new properties near to the Dartford factory and Mavis asked her elder brother, Norman, if Barry could see the plans.

"Yes, you two can choose which house you would like to purchase, and I will let you have the choice of wallpaper, but the two bungalows are already sold."

After some discussion and having looked around the site, they chose an end of terrace with its own garage in the back garden. Sometime later when the house was nearing completion, Norman said, "If you build or buy your own garage, I'll give you a hundred pounds off the purchase price."

Barry obtained some estimates for concrete slab and post garages and found it would cost around £100 plus erection. Barry rejected Norman's offer as he felt it would not look as nice as a brick-built garage.

Barry and Mavis moved in about six months later.

The two businesses were expanding, and Barry was spending most of his time estimating and visiting current and prospective clients. One day he received a letter from the Inland Revenue asking him to visit the local Tax Inspector. Having nothing to hide, he arrived at the appointed time and was shown into an office on the first floor above a Chinese restaurant. The room was painted dark grey with a large window overlooking a car park and furnished with a desk at which the Inspector, who Barry estimated to be in his mid-thirties, was sitting with his back against the wall. He got up as Barry entered and shook his hand.

"Thanks for coming, Mr Walker. Please take a seat," he said pointing to the chair facing the desk.

"It's a lovely day, you came down by car?" and not waiting for an answer added, "I suppose your wife is out shopping in her car? Wouldn't you like to be on your boat, today?"

"How did you know I have a boat?" asked Barry.

"It's registered at Lloyds!"

"Just a minute, I have not come here to chit chat, I've a lot of work to do," said Barry. "Why have you asked to see me?"

"According to our records you do not earn sufficient to own all these things."

Barry shot out of the chair and rushed around to the other side of the desk and looked over the Inspector's shoulder at the file notes. Looking down and seeing a salary of £1,500 a year, he said, "These figures are three years out of date!"

Barry walked out of the office without saying another word. He was not asked to visit the Inland Revenue again for many years.

Life was looking good for Barry. He had a new house, a new Seamaster boat, both he and Mavis had cars and a nice income from the two businesses. His companies – of which he owned 76% of the Dartford business and 50% of the Northfleet business with Dormer Anderson owning the balance, employing over 40 people and with a number of major clients – were making a name for themselves.

There were four terraced houses at the end of the cul-de-sac and Barry and Mavis had the one at the far end. In the front was a very small garden with a pond and a number of gold fish. Arriving home late one evening during the summer, as he put his key in the front door, Barry noticed there were a number of gold fish heads lying around the pond. "Have you seen the gold fish heads?" he said to Mavis as he walked in.

"Yes, it's that bloody cat of Pat and Wendy's," she said in a loud voice and looking very angry. "Go and complain to them."

"Oh, come on, it's a cat, that's what they do."

"I don't care, they have got to control it, go and see them."

"Bloody hell!" said Barry as he went out the front door.

He rang the bell two doors down and he waited, hoping Wendy would open the door. Wendy was beautiful: slim, dark hair, blue eyes and absolutely the best-looking woman in the court.

"Hello, Barry."

Barry almost dribbling, big smile, butter would not melt in his mouth, his eyes taking in such beauty, said, "Hello, Wendy. Sorry to disturb you but Mavis has sent me; it's about your cat, it's eaten our gold fish again."

"Pat, you had better come and look at this," she called out as she went through the door into the garden. *Damn*, thought Barry, *her old man's coming*.

As they walked along to view the fish heads, the door to Barry's house opened and Mavis stood in the doorway.

"Hello, Wendy, Pat, come on in and have a drink." Twenty minutes later, "Barry, go and get Ron and Jill next door."

As the evening wore on the men slowly became more pissed. Wendy and Pat had wobbled their way home. Mavis said, "Barry, take Ron out and walk him round the block, he's looking green and I don't want him being sick all over the floor."

"Yesss, dears."

Barry and Ron in their drunken state and unable to walk in a straight line, wandered around the roads and eventually found their way home.

The next day Ron went to work. Having been sick all up the stairs, Barry spent most of the night telephoning God down the big white telephone in the toilet and the rest of the day in bed. All caused by a cat and gold fish!

It was a Thursday in December 1966 and Barry rushed Mavis to West Hill Hospital Dartford. They were met by a rather tall dark nurse in maternity. Having waited for about three hours walking up and down sucking peppermints, Barry was told to go home as Mavis was unlikely to give birth until the next day.

The days went by and still no news. Mavis had been complaining of backache ever since she had been admitted. Barry found himself in the maternity waiting room early Sunday afternoon with another expectant father who was smoking and pacing around the room. Barry was pacing the other way, still sucking his peppermints, when a loud conversation was heard from out in the corridor.

"I told you to call me if the baby's head was visible! You should have called me. Now, call the Doctor!"

The two men, both looking very worried, looked at each other – one drawing on his cigarette, the other taking an extra hard suck on his peppermint – and both wondering whose wife was suffering.

At last, the sister came to the door holding a baby in each arm; she looked at both men before looking at Barry and then at the baby with long black hair. "This one is yours," she said.

Elizabeth Anne was born at 5pm on Sunday 18th December. It had been left too late for a caesarean and the Doctor had to use forceps, leaving Mavis's vaginal lips torn to pieces.

Barry was still working long hours and hardly ever got home to read his daughter a story before she went to bed, and never in the morning, as he was gone by 6am. When Elizabeth was just over 18 months old, Barry started to take time off on a Friday evening and just occasionally on a Friday afternoon. Mavis's mother would babysit so that he and Mavis could go to the Two Brewers Pub.

One Friday afternoon they were in the pub chatting to the locals one of whom was the Barclay Bank Manager from across the road. He was slowly becoming worse for wear, having been there some time. Suddenly, he collapsed and Barry, with the help of another fellow, laid him down on a long, soft seat.

"Iss neeed tooo talk tooo yous," he was trying to say. "Thee keys, theee wages, Isss have to get them ready…" He tried to get up but kept falling back down.

"What are you trying to say?" Barry said. "Do you mean that you have got the keys to get the money for a firm's wages?"

"Yesss."

*I had better get someone from the bank to come and collect them*, thought Barry.

He went across to the bank, went up to the first teller and said, "Do you have an Assistant Manager?"

"What do you want?"

Thinking he might get the Manager into trouble, Barry did not tell her about the drunken Manager at the pub. "Sorry, I must speak to the Assistant Manager or if you don't have one then the Chief Clerk. It is of the utmost importance. Please ask him to see me, now!"

Looking very suspicious, the teller got up passing two more tellers at their counters who, having overheard the conversation, were curious to know what was going on.

Barry could see the teller talking to a slim man in a dark suit at the back of the room who turned around with a curious look on his face. He came to one of the empty counters and spoke through the glass, "What can I help you with?"

Barry whispered, "I'm sorry, but your Manager has been taken ill. I understand that you have to pay out wages today and you will need the keys?"

"How do you know that?" said the man, keeping his voice down. "Where is he?"

"He's over the road in the pub." At last Barry got through to him and he came out a side door and followed him.

The Bank Manager was out for the count, and it took two of them to wake him. They found the keys in his side pocket. Barry said, "He can't go back to the bank like this; does he live nearby?"

"He lives in Gravesend."

"Let me have his address and we will get him home. You had better phone his wife to expect us."

Barry and one of the chaps from the pub took him home and carried him up the stairs and laid him on the bed.

Barry never came across him in the pub again!

# Chapter 23

# Changes

The phone rang one day. "Mr Walker, I have our Managing Director for you."

"You came to see me some time ago looking to quote for contracts. We have had a fire which has destroyed some of our storage facilities. Can you get over here tomorrow and give us a quote?" The firm was in Crawley and made flight simulators.

"Yes, I will be there around eleven."

Barry put down the phone and looked in his diary to check if he had to change any of his appointments. *Shit, I'm supposed to be at Mavis's Gran's funeral*, he thought. *Who is going to look after Elizabeth?*

After a row at home that evening, it was decided Barry would take his 18-month-old daughter with him to the appointment. Mavis made up a bag with nappies, drink, food and some toys to keep her happy. Barry was given his instructions to change her nappy and to look after her.

Arriving at the Crawley firm's offices, Barry took Elizabeth out of her car seat and put her in the pushchair. The office had glass doors on either side of a rotating central door. After a struggle he managed to get the pushchair into reception. At the desk were three lovely young ladies, obviously chosen for their looks and figures.

"Good morning, ladies, I have an appointment to give a quote on replacing some of the fire damaged items. But I also have a problem, as you can see," said Barry looking down at the baby in the pushchair.

All the girls came around the reception desk and started to baby talk to Elizabeth, cooing and making a fuss. "Isn't she lovely. Can I pick her up," they said, almost fighting each other for Elizabeth's attention.

The phone was ringing but not one of them seemed to notice.

"Ladies, I need to see the fire damage!"

"That's alright, you leave Elizabeth with us. I'll get someone to see you," said one.

Barry was there till late afternoon, measuring and asking questions and he completely forgot about his daughter. Suddenly, he remembered he had left her with the girls at reception and had forgotten to feed her. He quickly ran through to reception to find Elizabeth sitting on the floor happily playing with her toys.

"Sorry, girls, I was so busy that I forgot all about her. She hasn't had any food."

"We found some in her bag, she's eaten."

"Thanks very much, you have all been very kind."

"She has been the star attraction with everyone who has come in."

That evening when Barry got home with his little charge, he got one of the biggest bollockings of his life. "You haven't even changed her; she has been sitting in a wet nappy all day!" On and on and on for hours!

It happens to many a good business and White House businesses were not immune. Every so often Barry's companies would suffer with customers not paying their bills. Most of the time they could ride out the problem by chasing debt, getting the debtors to pay in instalments and, sometimes, increasing White House bank overdrafts.

Dormer Anderson had introduced a Polish company, based in the UK, who were designing a machine to manufacture wood panelling boards which were artificial tiles for fixing in bathrooms and kitchens.

It was agreed they could use disused offices at the Northfleet site.

The Polish company had been there for about eighteen months and were hoping to sell their first machine, not yet complete, to a French company. The two owners of the company had not been around for over ten days and invoices for nearly a year had not been paid, when Barry received a letter informing him that they were going into liquidation, owing White House companies over a hundred thousand pounds.

Barry was furious when he had a meeting with Dormer. "What are we going to do now; it could be the end of our companies? We will have to try the bank."

"They won't support us for an extra hundred thousand pounds," said Dormer.

Barry was looking very worried.

Domer, who had introduced the Poles, seemed to be a little smug when he said, "Can you put some money in?"

"Where am I going to get that amount of money, or anywhere near it?"

Taking some papers out of a drawer, Domer said, "I can arrange for the money if you hand over your shares in both companies to me."

"But then you will own the companies!"

"You can stay on your current salary and bring in the work," replied Dormer.

"What about getting my shares back?"

"You can buy them back over time."

Barry, in his worried state and more used to negotiating price with customers, agreed and signed the forms.

Within days he was on the phone chasing customers for more contracts and within months he had brought in a considerable amount of work, a lot of it very profitable. Several times he asked Domer if he could buy some of the shares back. Eventually, and getting fed up, Barry had a long chat with Mavis, and they agreed he should stick it out for a while longer.

Domer walked in to the Dartford office one day and said to Barry, "Do you speak German? I've been in touch with an American company and I'm after a franchise."

"A few words, why?" replied Barry. "What do they make and why German?"

"They produce water-proof cement for tunnels and basements. There is a tunnel exhibition in Bratislava, Czechoslovakia."

"They don't speak German there, and it's behind the Iron Curtain. How the hell would we get in?"

"For a start I would like you to go to Vienna and meet an Austrian Baron who will arrange a visa and take you across the border to the exhibition."

"But I've not seen this cement and don't know how to apply it. I would not have a clue!" said Barry.

Two weeks later, after a bust up with Mavis, Barry was on the train in London wondering how the hell he was going to get on with the language. *I've got myself in the shit this time with my bullshit,* he thought gloomily, when the carriage door opened and Domer climbed in.

"What are you doing here; I thought you were not coming?"

"I decided to join you."

Thinking about the Baron, Barry had imagined a tall, slim man in a Tyrolean suit. Instead, he was a short man, who spoke very good English, and who met them in a large American car.

After resting for a day to get over the journey, Barry and Dormer were taken down a small street where the Baron parked the car. Speaking to them before getting out, he said, "We are now going to get your visas and you will have to hand in your passports. I don't know how long this will take. Before we reach the queue, you will see standing on the other side of the road men in black leather jackets watching everyone. There will also be others in black inside the building. They are the SIB like the Stasi in East Germany, the secret police."

The place was full of people jostling with their passports held high trying to get to the front counters which were partly screened off so you could not see the person you were dealing with.

Eventually they drove out of Vienna towards the Czech border. The road was two lanes set on a ridge high above the surrounding fields which were devoid of trees. You could see for miles ahead and in the distance a very high wire fence with towers set at equal distances apart high above the fence.

About a mile or so before they got to the border, they were stopped by an Austrian border guard holding his gun with his trigger finger ready. The Baron spoke to him and was waved on. They were then in no-man's land. The Baron commented, "If you look at the Towers, without making it too obvious, you will see more of our black leather-coated friends watching us through their glasses."

Moving slowly, they approached the border. There were no other cars, trucks or people, just a guard in a different uniform with a gun, waving it to the three men to get out of the car. He pointed to a long green hut alongside a grey stone building. Feeling very nervous, they approached the hut to see two shutters placed at either end of the hut. The nearest one slid up and a hand came out. "Passport". Passports were handed over and Barry turned to look back at the Baron's American car as he noticed the guard walking around and looking inside.

Having waited for what seemed to be over half an hour, the furthest shutter slid up and another hand came out holding the passports.

Getting back into the car, the Baron said, "As I drive along this raised road watch the flashes as the sun catches on the binoculars of our leather-coated friends in the conning towers following our every move!"

Arriving in Bratislava and having not eaten for some hours, hunger set in. The Baron kept driving around trying to find a café. He stopped for a moment to turn to speak when the door of the car opened and a man said in English, "Are you lost?"

"No, we are looking for somewhere to eat."

"Let me show you," said the man getting into the car.

Following instructions, the Baron stopped outside of a rundown building. "You will find some food in there," said the man, pointing as he got out the car.

Having gone inside and sat down, a girl came up and spoke in Czech. The Baron replied in German. The girl had a blank look on her face and turned away, walking back to the counter. An old man, bent over and leaning on a stick, approached the table. "Coffee-e?" he said.

Nearly giving up, someone said, "Goulash." At last, they got through and were given bowls of very hot soup with dried bread.

Back in London, Barry made contact with contractors building a tunnel under the Thames for Royal Mail. He was asked if he could demonstrate the waterproof cement in the tunnel which was situated near Waterloo Station.

Once in the tunnel, he said to the chap in charge, "What's this tunnel for?"

"It's for a miniature railway to take the post to the South London sorting office."

# Chapter 24

# Agent Abroad

Barry was getting more and more restless. He had obtained a considerable amount of work for both companies but still had not been offered the opportunity to buy back any shares. He decided to leave but first he had to find a new job or set up a new business. Forever reading 'Engineering' and other publications, he found details of agents who bid for contracts and then farm them out the work to other companies to manufacture the parts. The agents made their money by paying the manufacturer less than the contact price. All he needed was an office and a 'Girl Friday' and, of course, some orders!

Barry faced a number of questions. Would he be able to secure sufficient work to make a living? He would have to find new customers; he could not go back to the White House customers. He also needed money to support the business until the new customers paid.

Without telling Mavis, he took out a second mortgage on their house and started to look for offices. To protect the family and to give his new venture more status, he formed a new company, Betan Limited, named after his daughter Elizabeth Ann which was also the name of his boat.

He found a modern, two-storey, glass-fronted office block attached to a warehouse. The office had its own entrance and parking area just off the main road in Welling Kent.

Over a period of time the business grew. Barry headhunted Ian (the works manager at White House) to assist him in finding contracts, Ian's father as bookkeeper, and an inspector to check the work of the subcontractors. But money was short; overheads had increased as had the business and his personal overdrafts. He took out a third mortgage on the house.

Barry still had his boat, moored on the River Medway at Rochester Cruising Club's moorings where he was club secretary. He would use it some weekends to go up river through the locks to Yalding and on an occasional club cruise. One Easter, the club arranged a trip up the Thames with about eight boats taking part. Working the tide, the boats moored up for the night at Codogan Pier next to Albert Bridge. Barry's motor cruiser 'Betan' had to moor alongside a 1930s cruiser.

Having sorted themselves out, a group of them went for a meal and on the way back walked down a pier, used by passenger cruisers, to look at the lights over the river. Looking over the river, they could see a boat moored in the middle, all lit up, music playing, dancing on the deck and people having a good time. A small launch left the side with one passenger and headed for the pier on which they were standing. As he was tying up to the pier, the driver said to the passenger, "Let me help you, Sir."

The launch was rocking, and the passenger could hardly stand, wobbling all over the place, drunk. At the third attempt the passenger managed to grab hold of a metal bar to support himself as he walked unsteadily up the slope. "You OK, Frankie?" said Barry.

"Who was that?" asked one from the group.

"Frankie Howard."

It was pitch black at 5 o'clock in the morning and Mavis started to shake Barry. "Wake up," she said in a whisper. "Someone's walking about on deck!" Half asleep, Barry started to put on a dressing gown as the boat continued to rock and made his way on deck.

"Sorry to wake you, we were trying to be quiet; we need to catch the tide!"

"I'll come and help."

Barry walked across the deck of the cruiser to which his boat was moored and took one of the ropes from a most beautiful young lady. He jumped on to the quay.

"Have I seen you before?" he asked as he looked across to the man, whose voice he seemed to recognise, trying to see in the dark.

"I'm Raymond Baxter; you may have seen me on TV in 'Tomorrow's World'."

"Where are you going at this time in the morning?"

"My boat is one of the Little Ships that went across to Dunkirk. A few of us Little Ships are off down river calling in at a couple of places and ending up at Rochester Cruising Club on Monday."

"Well, well, these boats you are letting off the moorings, including mine, are all from the club and we will be back to meet you and for getting me up at this time in the morning you can buy me a beer in the bar!"

The following Monday they met in the bar at the club and true to his word Raymond brought Barry a beer and the beautiful young lady turned out to be his 15-year-old daughter!

Rochester Cruising Club was based just below the Castle in the River Medway. Some of the club boats were moored at the end of the pier and the rest moored on trots out in the river. They were tied to large, thick buoys – like space hoppers – which in turn were chained to the riverbed. To get out to your boat you would hail Jonny Oliver to take you across in his launch. Jonny, who worked part time for the club, had no arms below his elbows and a club foot. He was a very educated man who spoke with an upper middle-class accent and would pick up Elizabeth in his short arms and sit her in his launch. Jonny lived on a tug boat out in the river and used to get the odd towing job.

Mavis's brother Ralph and his wife invited themselves for a trip on the boat one weekend. Barry called Jonny over to give them all a lift over to the boat.

"Remember, Ralph, there is only ONE captain on a boat, so don't touch anything unless I tell you."

Jonny ferried everyone to the boat and, holding the side with his foot to keep it steady, told Ralph and his wife to get on board. Mavis and Barry had a simple system; she would go up to the bow and unhook the bow rope from the buoy. Barry would start the engine, but not put it in gear, and remove the rope from the stern buoy.

"Ralph, I'm just going to start the engine. Would you take the stern line off the buoy, don't drop the rope into the water."

What did he do, drop the rope! There was a hell of a racket. The engine started to whine, and Barry quickly turned the engine off.

"Ralph, you BLOODY IDIOT, I told you not to drop the rope!" The rope had wrapped itself around the prop. Barry had forgotten that his brother-in-law was accident prone.

That was the end of the day out and Jonny was called to take Ralph and his wife off. Jonny came back and said to Barry, "I'll tow you over to Wingete's Wall, it has a shelf which dries out at low tide, and you can go over the side with a sharp knife and cut the rope off."

"Thanks."

Barry moored up leaving the ropes slack so that as the tide went down the boat was not left hanging on the ropes but resting on the riverbed. They had to wait, adjusting the ropes as the water receded to keep the boat level. At last, she settled on the riverbed.

With his wellies on and sharp knife in hand, Barry slowly lowered himself over the side.

"It's past lunchtime and I've got those pork chops out, I'll cook them while you are doing that," said Mavis.

There was not much mud; the shelf was man-made for the boats to settle on at low tide for them to unload timber for the wood yard.

The rope had wrapped around the prop three or four times and Barry started to cut it away. Suddenly the boat moved, tipping about 10 or 15 degrees away from the wall. CRASH, followed by an almighty SCREAM! The ropes tightened, holding her from going over on her side and Barry moved from under FAST, shouting to Mavis, "WHAT HAPPENED?"

"The chops have flown out of the oven and hit the wall on the other side and fallen on the floor."

"Well, pick them up and we will eat them later."

Barry walked through the door, having just arrived home from the office, when Mavis said, "We've had an invitation to a wedding."

"Who's getting married?"

"My cousin Colin, he's marrying a Dutch girl and we have been invited to the wedding in Holland."

"Is Elizabeth invited?"

"Yes."

"Do they know that she is only eighteen months old?"

"Of course they do; we will be staying in one of Petra's relation's homes."

Two days before the wedding, Barry drove down to Dover in his Jag loaded up with baby clothes, food, toys, toilet seat and the cuddly vest, the three of them ready to make the journey to Holland. Having settled Mavis and Elizabeth into the Dutch house, Barry continued to struggle up and down the narrow winding stairs with the suitcases. Each time he went to the car to get the next case he was surrounded by a group of people looking at the car and asking questions in English.

Two fellows, one rather rotund and short with receding hair and the other slim with fair hair, taller and looking younger asked Barry, "What do you do?"

Barry thought for a moment, knowing that they would not understand what a manufacturing agent is, and replied, "I have an engineering company."

They spoke to each other in Dutch and one of them said, "Would you be interested in doing business with an Indonesian company?"

"What kind of business?"

"We are stewards with KLM, and we meet many businessmen when we fly in and out of Indonesia and we have to stay over between flights."

"Here's my card; give me a call if you have anything in the engineering line."

About three months later, Barry received a telephone call at home. "Mr Walker, there is a very important man from Indonesia coming to Holland in two days, can you come over to meet him?"

"Who is he?"

"He is connected with the Government, and he is looking to purchase items in Holland and the UK."

"OK, I will be there in the next two days; where shall we meet?"

"Just call this number and give me your flight details and we will meet you at the airport."

Business was difficult and money was tight, in fact very tight, but ever ready to chase up more business, Barry arrived some days later and was greeted by his two contacts.

"The VIP has arrived, and we are just awaiting an appointment to see him, so we have booked you a room in the Hilton."

They spent all day over lunch, coffee and kicking their heels, with one of them trying to track down the VIP on the hotel's phones. Barry was getting more and more frustrated. In late afternoon they had a message that the VIP would meet them in the hotel at 7pm. Nearer the time they all stood looking through the plate glass windows awaiting his arrival.

"Here he is," said one of the Dutch stewards pointing out of the window.

Looking out of the window, Barry could see a slim man of medium height wearing a trilby hat pulled over one side of his head slightly shading his eyes with his shoulders bent forward and a cigarette dangling from his mouth. He walked with a swagger, almost like a ship rolling in a slight sea. He reminded Barry of a character from a TV serial, Arthur Daly.

After the introductions and more coffee, the VIP, who never took his hat off, looked at Barry with bloodshot eyes and said, "The meeting is set up for tomorrow."

After he had left, the three of them sat over a drink and Barry said, "Why has he kept us waiting so long?"

"He's been shacked up with two birds all night and this morning!"

The following day Barry was met by one of the stewards and taken to a small house in the suburb where he was introduced to three people. The chap who had taken him to this venue proceeded to leave the room. Barry had expected to be seated around a table to conduct business, however, they all sat around in armchairs.

One short Indonesian man then offered Barry a seat and as he sat down, he noticed a Chinaman sitting in an ornate high chair to his right. The chair was dark wood with gold dragons carved on the back and arms. The man was sitting with his hands together in a praying position and his face was expressionless, the only one who had not been introduced.

The three men began asking questions about the business and Betan Limited. This lasted for some time and the Indonesian began to tell Barry about his friendship with Prince Phillip. He took out a large photograph of himself standing next to Prince Phillip with a dead Tiger lying on the ground next to them.

As the Chinaman had not said a word, Barry assumed he could not speak English, but he suddenly said in a loud English voice, waving his hands, "Mr Walker, we can do business."

After the three had shaken hands, Barry was shown out.

# Chapter 25

# Betan

Barry's agency company Betan Limited was named after his daughter Elizabeth Anne, as was his boat.

It was two months later and Betan Limited was still having problems: the bills were mounting up, money was very short, and Barry had not heard from the Indonesians. Then a letter arrived from Holland to say that a trade minister from Indonesia and his assistants were coming to visit and would like to be booked in a nearby hotel. Enclosed with the letter was a list of items they wished to purchase which totalled in value over one million pounds. The list included Bedford trucks and generators.

In those days there were no hotels within a reasonable distance of the office and Barry had to book the five of them in to a large pub with rooms above.

Barry started to phone various companies to try and get prices and details of delivery but kept coming up against problems. "Can't supply you, you will have to go talk to our agent." He felt as though he was banging his head against a brick wall.

He received a call to meet with one of the minister's staff to discuss some of the minister's requirements. "Can you arrange for some girls for tonight, say four, and the minister would like a thousand pounds."

That was it, Barry knew he was getting nowhere, and it was going to cost him a lot of money. He told the staff member he could not help, and they left.

Barry was still left with a hotel bill of over £1,000!

The company still had one possible large contract which, if the company machining the parts could get the sample accepted, would mean a very profitable job.

Barry flew to Cologne in Germany taking a very small round headed sample in his case. He was taking it to the inspectors at KHD, a manufacturer of large trucks, for approval. He arrived at the works gate early and spoke in English to a one-legged chap who was sitting in what looked like a sentry box who told Barry that the inspectors had not yet arrived. As he waited, he watched the other workers arriving, many in shorts and carrying briefcases, and some with only one arm. Barry assumed that they had been injured during the war and was surprised that everyone he had met was very friendly and helpful.

Finally, he met with the inspectors only to have the part he had carried from England rejected.

On his return to the office Barry sat for some time trying to work out a solution to his and the firm's financial problems. The firm was broke, and he was up to his eyes in debt, with three mortgages and many bills unpaid.

Betan's staff of four had to be told that the company was closing, and they would be losing their jobs.

After his loss of the engineering companies to Dormer Anderson, Barry had taken some time to study more details on legal matters relating to companies. Over the years he had built up a relationship with his Bank Manager, Tony Pine of NatWest, but Barry was concerned that if he discussed it with the Bank Manager before he had devised a plan, the Bank would pull the plug.

Decision made! He would put the company into voluntary liquidation, set the date for the meeting, place advertisements in the papers and then go and see Tony at the Bank. He then had to face Mavis and tell her he had forged her signature to obtain the two extra mortgages to put into the business which would now be lost.

Arriving home, having spent the journey trying to think how he was going to tell Mavis, he put the key in the door as Mavis said, "You're home early," as she came in from the kitchen. "What's wrong, you look terrible."

Barry was almost in tears, his face white, choking as he said, "I'm sorry, I'm sorry, I should not have done it." Breaking down, he collapsed on the stairs sobbing. Mavis had never seen him like this before and put her arms around him. "What's the matter, what you have done, just tell me."

Having told Mavis the truth, giving her all the details of liquidating the company and explaining that they would not have to pay the company's debts, Barry and Mavis decided they would have to sell the house in order to pay off the mortgages.

Barry met with Tony Pine, his Bank Manager at Southwark, and explained the details as to why he was putting the company into voluntary liquidation. Having become friends, Tony was understanding even though the company overdraft was a loss to the bank and would go down on the record during his watch as Manager.

"Whilst the Bank will have to accept the company loss, there is still the question of your personal overdraft. How do you propose to pay that off?"

"Well, I have thought about that, I'll sell my boat."

"Fine, I won't put a time limit as to when you will clear it. I have every faith that you will make it one day and I will be there to support you."

The day came for the voluntary liquidation meeting which was to be held in the downstairs office. Barry set out a table at the front of the room from which he would address the creditors to give an account as to why he was putting the company into voluntary liquidation and to answer any questions.

He had his notes prepared and was walking up and down feeling every worried. He expected lots of worrying questions. Time ticked by, he kept looking at his watch. *Where are they?* he thought, expecting at least four or five to turn up. Having waited over two hours he gave up, closed and locked the door and went home.

He had not yet reached his personal overdraft limit and having put the house on the market, he had a little leeway to find money for food. He had been an employee of the company and was now out of work, so he signed on at the local labour exchange which gave a small boost to his income. After a lengthy discussion, Barry and Mavis decided to look for a house further out into Kent near to where they kept the boat. But there still remained the problem of obtaining a mortgage!

During his apprenticeship he met a chap who had just come back from the Korean War and had been wounded in the leg. Ron had worked the centre lathe next to Barry and they became friends and had kept in touch. Ron and two friends had set up their own engineering company which was still going strong. Barry decided to approach Ron to see if he would be prepared to give him a reference in the hope it would help him obtain a mortgage.

Mavis and Barry found a house at Cuxton, a village overlooking the River Medway. The property was built on a bank looking down river. It looked like a bungalow from the front and a three-storey house from the back. The property was in two parts: just over a half an acre with a house on it and another half an acre suitable for a second house for which the owner wanted an extra £500.

With a mortgage, Barry could afford to purchase the house but not the land next door. However, he felt he could make a profit if he could buy the land and sell it on. He wondered who would lend him £500.

Barry approached his solicitor who said "YES" and the land was sold six months later for £2,650!

Looking to find a job or start another business, Barry was walking along Strood High Street one day when he came across an empty shop. Through the window he could see glass display units along the side walls where cameras had previously been displayed. Walking round the back, Barry saw a slightly rough area in which two cars could be parked. If he could obtain a lease, what could he do with it?

That weekend when Barry was cleaning his boat moored at Rochester Cruising Club, just below the Castle, on the next berth was his friend Bill.

"Fancy a drink, Barry?"

"That sounds good, shall I come across?"

"I'll get the bottle out."

After they had talked about the club and the upcoming boating events, Bill asked, "Have you found a job yet?"

"No, but I have looked at an empty shop near yours." Bill had a shoe repair and handbag shop.

"What would you do with it?"

"I don't know, and I don't have much money to refurbish and buy any stock."

"What about a ladies' hairdresser? My mother has just closed her shop because of a fire but she managed to save the hairdryers, four of them, would you like them?"

"How much would she want for them?"

"Nothing, you can have them."

# Chapter 26

# Try Again

Barry and Mavis discussed how they could use the shop. They would need a good hairdresser and advertised for staff. Barry set about redecorating and they both gave the shop a good clean. But they were stuck; what would they do with all the glass wall cabinets? Suggestions went back and forth. "I know," said Barry, "when all those ladies are sitting there having their hair done, they could be looking at a display of children's clothes in the cabinets!"

The next Sunday morning Barry and Mavis were off to London to the warehouses and picked up some stock. Linked to and behind the shop were two large rooms in one of which Barry had put a desk and chair and used as his office. Sitting there one day and feeling bored, he mulled over what to do to do with the space to try make some more money. He picked up the local paper from his desk and started to glance through the small ads. "I know, why not start up as a jobbing builder. If I get a couple of lads and advertise fencing, gates, drives and ground work, I could do the estimating and they could carry out the work." A month later Barry had two strong lads, a large old Austin van and three jobs on the go!

The hairdressing shop was doing well, and the chief stylist was well liked by customers and the two other staff. Mavis and Barry promoted her to Manageress and let the flat on the ground floor of their house to her.

The jobbing building side of the businesses was also going from strength to strength. One day the lads approached Barry: "Baz, do you know of any flats to rent?"

"No, but I'll ask at the cruising club."

Some days later he was sitting at the bar of the club chatting to Bill who had given him his mother's hairdryers to start the hairdressers.

"How are the businesses doing?" asked Bill.

"Not bad!"

"Could you do with some more work?"

"I'm always interested in extra work!"

"Well, we need a new shop front, care to give us a price? And while you are at it, you could quote for a new fence around the club house, but that would have to go to the club committee."

"Thanks, Bill. While you are here, you don't happen to know of any flats to let?"

"Well, there's the top flat in my shop, who is it for?"

"My two lads who work on the building side; in fact, they would put in the new shop front for you – if I get the contract."

Some two or three months later the two lads had settled in the flat and Barry overheard them talking, while they were having a tea break at the back of his shop.

"Jeez, that was a session last night, both of us fucking her, then she gave me a blow job and you kissed her immediately after – how could you!"

Barry was starting to get bored and thinking to himself he was never going to be wealthy at this rate. He started reading the local paper; he always ran an advert to try and pick up general building work. Looking through the 'Situations Vacant' to check the rates his competitors were paying their staff, the word 'HAMBRO' in capital letters caught his eye. He had just finished reading a paperback entitled 'The City', each chapter was on the history of a merchant bank, with Hambro Bank having their own chapter.

The advertisement stated that Hambro were looking for people to represent them and to apply for an interview at their offices in Maidstone. Barry applied. It turned out to be Hambro Life Assurance which had started trading in 1972. It was now early in 1972.

After three interviews, he discovered it was commission only but there was a drawdown for the first three months as an advance against future commission. He attended the training course on 10 April.

As an incentive to sell, the company set targets each year which, if met, qualified representatives to go to their overseas convention. The very first was to be in Istanbul in September 1973. Barry qualified to attend in just five months, and he could take Mavis.

After a delay of some seven hours at Heathrow – when Mavis had threatened to go home if there was any further delay – they eventually arrived at the Hilton Hotel in Istanbul. There were meetings for the Associates, as the sales people were called, and outings for their wives.

The ladies were taken on an escorted tour of the Casbah; they were told to keep together and were warned they would be pestered to buy, and men would try to touch them. Mavis became friendly with Pat, the wife of another Associate from Maidstone, and on the way back to the hotel they discussed how cheap the leather goods were. "I'd like to get a leather suit made if we have time," said Pat.

The courier overheard the conversation and said, "Most of the shops will make you a suit in a day; you go in and have your measurements taken in the morning and pick it up next day."

Mavis agreed to go with Pat the next day and they hired a taxi. After spending an hour in the shop while Pat's measurements were taken, they asked the staff if they could order a taxi to take them back to the Hotel. "Five minutes, outside," said one in broken English.

Mavis and Pat went out of the shop and were almost immediately surrounded by Turkish men – all of them dark, smelly and needing a shave – trying to pinch their bums. The taxi arrived and Pat looked in the cab, "I'm not getting in there, it's filthy!"

"Bugger that, I don't care if it's an ox cart, just bloody well get in before this lot rape us!" cried Mavis.

Later that evening Mavis told Barry of their experience. "Do you mean to tell me I could have swapped you for a camel," said Barry with a grin on his face. "Trouble is I wouldn't be able to get it on the plane."

In order to find new clients Hambro placed a number of advertisements in the national newspapers. In addition, they ran courses in telephone cold calling and asking for introductions after meeting someone or a sale. There was a standard presentation kit and after asking a number of questions, the associate would fill in an illustrated form and present to the prospective client or clients.

Replies to the advertisements expressing interest were passed on to the managers of the nearest branch who then gave them to the associates. The managers had to decide who they should give the leads to: the associate who was better at converting to a sale or the new associates to help them get started. All managers had targets to achieve in order to increase their income.

It was winter and with many people working during the day, Barry had to phone in the evening for appointments. It was the time of the mini skirt, and he had an appointment for 8.30pm in Sidcup.

It was a pitch-black night and after driving around trying to find the street, Barry stopped outside a five-storey building which was in compete darkness. He walked down the path and pressed the door bell, waiting. He stepped back, looked up and thought to himself, *This is like a Hitchcock movie, a bit creepy.* After ringing twice more and walking back to look up to the windows again to see if any lights were on, he was about to give up when a light came on at the very top. He waited, watching the lights in the windows as they slowly came on. Someone was coming down the stairs. Moments later the door opened and standing there was a young lady of about nineteen or twenty in a very short mini skirt, one of the most beautiful girls he had ever seen.

"I've come to see Mrs Jones," said Barry in a shaky voice. "She replied to one of our adverts," and at the same time thinking that this must be Mrs Jones's daughter.

"That's me, Miss Jones, do come in. Follow me, I'm afraid it's at the top of the stairs," she said with a lovely smile. Barry was melting.

Barry, briefcase in hand, proceeded to follow her. He could not help but look up, finding himself peering straight up her skirt, looking at lovely slim legs and tiny frilly panties. He began to get out of breath, partly because of the view and partly because of the ten flights of stairs! She did not seem bothered; she was almost showing him everything! Barry reached the top, bent double, trying to get his breath. She stood there, breathing a little heavily with her small, firm breasts rising and falling in a very seductive way with a lovely grin on her face.

"Do follow me."

As she walked along the passage Miss Jones said, "I hope you don't mind but we are not into furniture," and pushed open a door. The room had bare boards with just a mattress on the floor. Sitting on the mat with his back leaning against the wall was a young man of about twenty. "Please sit down," she said, pointing to the other end of the mattress. After introductions and questions, Barry took a leaflet out and started to enter figures. The young lady took the leaflet and turned around to face her boyfriend, sticking her bum in the air four inches from Barry's face. Barry became very aroused! He laid his case over his lap.

It was another very dark evening and Barry was in a tree-lined avenue with grass verges. It was pitch black and he had to get out of his car and walk down driveways to see the house numbers. Having found the house he was looking for, he rang the doorbell. Introducing himself he was invited into the lounge.

Part-way through the presentation, Barry pulled a face as he turned to his paperwork. *What's that smell?* he said to himself. *It smells like shit! The house seems very clean; it must be him sitting next to me.*

Having finished the presentation Barry said goodbye and got into his car to go home. Driving home the smell seemed to follow him and on arrival he could at last see by the light under the carport. There was shit everywhere all over the pedals, over the mat and down the side of the door. Barry and Mavis spent some hours cleaning it up and it took two to three days for the smell to go. He had stepped on it in the grass looking for the house number. Barry never phoned or went back, he was too embarrassed!

Together with some of the other top associates, Barry was invited to dinner by some of the Hambro Directors. They met in a top London hotel for drinks before dinner and were swapping stories before going into eat. As time went on, they were called into dinner and Barry noticed there were not many associates. Looking at the seating plan, he found himself on the centre table leg of the three legs up against the top table.

The meal progressed with the appropriate wine for each course and the talk became louder as more drink was consumed. Barry moved his foot sharply to his left. CLANK!

*Christ! What was that?* thought Barry. He looked up at Jocelyn Hambro, the Chairman of Hambros Bank, one of the founders of Hambro Life.

"Sorry, Sir," said Barry.

"Careful, Barry," said Mark Weinberg sitting next to Jocelyn.

Barry then realised he had just kicked Jocelyn's tin leg. He had lost his leg in Normandy during the Second World War.

# Chapter 27

# In the Limelight

Barry was now one of the top three associates in the Maidstone Branch and in the top 20 of the UK based on the monthly figures. He decided to sell off the hairdressers and give all his attention to the sale of financial products. He spent more time on developing marketing ideas and presentations in order to build a client base. He also spent some time preparing a personalised fact-find and report to present to prospective clients. He never put these in the post but presented them on his second visit, allowing clients to read through and ask questions.

He was in the office one day when the Manager, Mac Macintyre, approached him. "Barry, have you got a moment?" Barry went into the Manager's office.

"You've have been noticed!" said Mac.

"What do you mean?"

"Well, the Directors want you to give a talk to all the partners in London."

"Bloody hell!"

"But first they are sending down a camera to record your talk and then they will get back in touch. Are you prepared to do it?"

"Yes."

Barry spent hours not only trying to think of what to say, but also practicing before recording his talk. About a week later he was told that that his talk was acceptable, and he was to attend the conference in the Grosvenor Hotel Ball Room in Park Lane, London.

The big day came, and Barry sat on the platform alongside Tim Walker one of the Directors. Tim was smoking a fat cigar and blowing smoke across the stage.

Next to Barry sat a chap from Northern Ireland who was to speak before him. Some moments later the Northern Ireland chap was introduced to over one thousand guests in the room and began to speak. Within minutes he had the whole audience falling about in laughter and this carried on to the end of his session. Barry felt like tearing his notes up and walking out. How could he follow that, his talk was serious with no jokes?

The introduction came and nervously Barry slowly got up to address the audience. Well, they did not boo him, his first speech!

At dinner that evening in the Dorchester Hotel he sat next to Mark Weinberg (later to become Sir Mark Weinberg) the Managing Director and they got talking. Mark took out his pocket diary on the front of which was stuck a post-it note. He then took out a red pen and scribbled a note. He put the pen away and turning his diary over, took out a black pen and scribbled a note on another post-it note. When Barry asked, he explained, "The red notes at the front are the urgent things to be done as soon as possible and the black notes have to be done but are not so urgent."

On the marketing side Barry was aiming for the higher wealth clients, medium-size firms, accountants, solicitors, top managers and local doctors. To make himself known, find new clients and recognising that the professionals were always looking for new business, he asked some of them to speak at seminars, which Barry would arrange. He decided to hold a seminar at the Great Danes Hotel in Maidstone and arranged for a speaker from Head Office to talk on investment, together with a solicitor and an accountant.

The evening went well, and Barry now had a list to follow up for business. He had arranged for the main speaker to stay overnight in the hotel and a small group of speakers, guests and two other associates stayed on for a few drinks. A 'few' turned into 'many', even after the bar closed. Barry started to put the miniature bottles of whisky in his pocket.

One of the accountants was getting drunk – quickly! He got up from his seat trying to say he was going home. He staggered out to the car park with Barry and two others following. Having dropped his keys twice while trying to put them in the car door, all three of them tried to stop him. A fight nearly broke out as they tried to hold him and take his keys away, but the accountant won and drove off.

Barry said to the remaining two, who were not staying at the hotel, "It's time to go. Leave your cars here; you are going to stay at my house tonight."

It was nearly three in the morning and there were no other vehicles on the north bound carriageway of the M20. Barry drove at just over ninety miles per hour before turning off to Snodland. As he slowed down going into the thirty miles an hour zone, Barry glanced into his rear-view mirror. He noticed a police car was just behind.

"Fellows, we are about to be stopped by the police and it smells like a brewery in this car, just stay quiet."

The police car flashed its lights indicating for him to stop. Barry pulled over and stopped the car. He got out. He guessed what was coming.

"Good morning, Sir," said the policeman as he approached. "We have been following you and at one time we could not record your speed, it was well over a hundred miles per hour."

The policeman sniffed. "You have been drinking, breathe into this," he said as he handed a breathalyser to Barry. Looking at the result, he said. "You are over the limit. I'm sorry, Sir, you cannot drive any further; we will have to take you to West Malling Police Station."

"But what is going to happen with these two in the back of my car; they are both drunk and I refused to let them drive to their homes? I only live just down the road at Cuxton."

The two policemen had a quick discussion. "You get in the back of the police car and my colleague will drive your car to your home."

It was about a mile to Barry's home, and they arrived a few minutes later. However, what the officer driving Barry's car did not know was that his home was below the road level, down a steep slope going back parallel to the way he had come. The officer made two attempts at driving the car down the drive. Barry got out of the other police car and said, "Shall I do it?"

"No! You are not allowed to drive."

Mavis had been standing at the side door looking very, very, worried watching the attempt to get the car down the drive. She gave a shout to Barry who was looking over the wall. "Where are you going? When will you be back?"

"I have to go to West Malling Police Station, and I don't know how long I shall be."

On the way to West Malling, Barry started chatting to the two police officers. He asked them about their jobs and the shifts they worked. They became quite friendly, and they asked him what he did and where he had been that evening. One of them, the one not driving, turned to Barry and said, "We will not charge you for speeding but unfortunately you are charged with drink driving."

Barry said his thanks and realised that being friendly paid.

Some weeks later the Magistrate sentenced him, and, having heard his story, he was fined £25 and given a one-year driving ban.

As for the drunken accountant, he arrived home safely but could not get his key in the door which was then opened by his wife. He duly fell in and fell asleep on the floor. His wife threw a blanket over him!

The next week's local paper had a headline on an inside page, 'A FRIEND IN DEED' referring to Barry helping his drunken friends.

Ron an ex-boxer, became Barry's personal driver. He had the use of the car when Barry did not need it and being a golf fanatic with a handicap of two, managed to play quite a lot.

The years were ticking by and Barry as a member of the top sales club, a President Falcon, had been at another branch training others. On his return to the Maidstone office, he was approached by Ted. "Have you seen the paper?"

"No, what paper?"

"The Daily Telegraph. Look at this, in the situations vacant section."

In a large advertisement, Hambro Life were looking for a manager for a new office in Hayes near Bromley. The contact was one of the Directors and Barry rang and asked, "Why did you not consider me for the position?"

"I didn't know you would be interested. Come up and see me."

The premises turned out to be an old bank in the High Street with a large reception area, the counter still in place, a very large Manager's office, a massive safe and a large room at the back.

Barry took over the branch some weeks later and began recruiting. He was set targets by the Area Director which included associates on commission only (with a drawdown against future commission payments) and a secretary. He had to give further training after the associates came back from the initial basic training.

Barry's sales were part of the monthly branch figures. Some year or so later he was called into the area office to be told that his contribution at some 40 to 50% was too much and that he had to reduce his percentage and the associates must increase theirs.

Barry was angry – it would mean reducing his income and having to spend more time taking associates on visits, teaching and lecturing. He resigned as a manager and went back to the Maidstone Branch!

However, Barry was not happy. After having his own office, he now had to find an empty desk whenever he came into the branch, and he spent more and more time working from home.

## Chapter 28

## Welcome Wagon

At the bottom of the stairs, in the conservatory, at his home in Cuxton was the hall leading to the flat which Mavis and he had let. The manageress of their shop had occupied this for some time. At the other end, partly under the garage, was a very small room just big enough to take a desk and chair. Barry thought that if he used this room for a part-time secretary, she could use the side entrance without coming through the house. He placed an advert in the local paper.

Having interviewed four ladies, he chose a very nice lady from the village who agreed to work three days a week during school hours. She lasted just six weeks having found a better job. Being in need, he took on the next best lady to help out. She was not so smart, what one might call a bit scruffy, the odd hole in her tights, and a bit too chatty.

One evening, Barry was at a prospective client's house and asking questions in order to prepare their report.

"How long have you lived here, very long?"

"No, we only moved in two months ago."

"How are you finding it in the area, the neighbours and the shops?"

"It's been very good, that lady from Welcome Wagon, she was very helpful with her basket of information."

"Welcome Wagon, I've not heard of them, what do they do?"

"Well, from what she told me they got our name from the Estate Agents, and they put together train timetables, school details, maps of the town centre, local services and cards from various trades and gave us lots of information."

Barry got in touch with Welcome Wagon and met two ladies to discuss them representing him in their areas. He arranged to pay them a little extra for more information after they had visited the new people.

A gentleman living in Chislehurst replied to an advert about pensions. Barry called early one evening and was shown into the kitchen. After introductions Barry started to ask his normal questions to establish the facts in order make recommendations and prepare his report. Having established he was self-employed, Barry asked, "What is your net profit?"

"I'm not telling you."

"Then what is your highest rate of tax? I cannot advise you without some information."

The conversation went on for some time with the prospective client refusing to answer Barry's questions.

Barry bent down to the side of the kitchen table to pick up his open briefcase, closed it, and as he got up said, "I am sorry, I am not prepared to help you," and proceeded to walk towards the door.

"Wait!"

From his fact-find Barry identified that in some cases there was a need for other companies' products as sometimes clients would request additional products. He also found that in his quest to give assistance he was asked to provide help in arranging loans and introductions to banks. Barry decided to set up another small business to prepare reports to submit to lenders and to make introductions to other professionals such as solicitors and accountants.

Some months previously Barry had employed a new secretary. She turned up for the interview with a cold. Her red nose and sniffles made him feel a bit sorry for her. He asked her to take a small test by typing two letters for him, which she did very neatly and very quickly, far better and quicker than the other girl. Both had children but the new lady, Joan, had an eighteen-month-old little girl and worked part time. Joan was by far the more professional and was to become Barry's 'right-hand man', so much so that the other woman used to call her pet!

Barry asked Joan if she would like to be a partner in a new business which he was calling 'Dual Services'. At first, she refused. Barry explained why he was forming it and what services the business would offer and also explained that she would be self-employed. This was the sticking point. Joan had always been employed on PAYE and did not understand how she would pay her tax. Barry took her along to meet one of his contacts, a Chartered Accountant, who answered all her questions. She finally agreed which pleased Barry as he wanted to retain her to work with him in all his businesses.

Barry had become very successful and started to make improvements and additions to his house. He added two more rooms one above the other. The lower one became a changing room for the new swimming pool which extend out into the new patio area with steps leading down to the garden. He filled in the pond in the old patio as all the fish had been eaten by a heron! The pool and the new patio looked out over the River Medway.

Late one summer evening Barry and Mavis were sitting in the lounge watching television. "Do you fancy a Chinese, Mavis?"

"Yes, but I better go, you've had a drink."

"OK."

Sometime later Barry was still watching TV when he thought he heard his name called. No, I must be dreaming he thought and went back to watching his programme. A few seconds later he heard it again, this time a little louder. Barry got up and walked through the kitchen, opened the side door and looked out to the car port, no car. Then he heard his name called again, even louder. He walked back down the hall to the front door and opened it to be faced with the roof of Mavis's car. The car was lying on its side having fallen over the side of the drive on to the path which led to the front door.

Mavis was trapped inside, lying against the door on the driver's side which was lying on the concrete path.

Barry immediately climbed on to the side of the car, standing with his legs braced apart, and pulled as he turned the door handle. Reaching in he said to Mavis, "Are you alright?"

"I think I've broken my arm."

"Let me get you out first and we will have a look."

Lying on his stomach along the side of the car he reached in and released her seat belt. Wrapping his arms around Mavis he began to pull her out, thinking that he had better move fast as he could smell PETROL!

At that moment his neighbour appeared carrying a fire extinguisher.

"Don't spray it yet; if we are careful, it may not catch fire."

"What happened?" asked Barry.

"I was in the middle of the road, turning to come down the drive, when a lad on a motorbike hit the front of the car and went flying over the bonnet pushing the car over the side."

Looking up Barry could see a lad sitting on the wall. He was holding his right arm, groaning. Leaving Mavis for a moment, Barry ran up the drive to check if the lad was alright.

"Are you alright?" he said looking at the white-faced lad.

"Yes, I'm sorry, I'm sorry."

"Where is your bike?"

"Over there," said the lad, pointing along the road.

"I had better get that off the road before it causes another accident," said Barry as he noticed the bike had learner plates.

"Can you phone for an ambulance for the lad while I take Mavis inside, check her over and phone the lad's father," said Barry to his neighbour.

Thirty minutes later Barry was seen looking inside the car trying to rescue the Chinese food!

Barry's education in the industry was improving all the time with at least three or four courses and exams each year. Every year there were two conventions – for which he qualified – in cities and countries around the world. In order to remain in one of the top two clubs in Hambro Life, Barry worked late in the evenings (on one occasion till two in the morning) and at weekends. There was also a one-day convention for all the partners, as the sales staff were called, in top London five-star hotels, followed by a dinner and cabaret for the top partners. The personal assistants of the very top partners were invited to the one-day conventions in London, but not the dinner and cabaret. However, Barry arranged, at his expense, for Mavis and Joan to have dinner together and a show. On their return, they would look in the cabaret room and, standing just inside the doors, see some of the acts.

On the home front, Mavis and Barry's daughter Elizabeth returned from the village junior school one day and Mavis asked, "What did you do at school today, Elizabeth?"

"I played in the sandpit, and do you know, Mummy, that little boy John threw a chair at teacher!"

When Barry arrived home Mavis told him what had happened at the school, and they had a talk about Elizabeth's education. They decided to phone St. Andrew's private school in Rochester to see if the school would take her.

Barry and Mavis were asked to attend an interview with Elizabeth. Commander Starkey asked questions of them all, and said, "I would like you to bring Elizabeth to school on Saturday morning and leave her here on her own with some of my other children. You can pick her up at twelve thirty and when I have made my assessment, I will call you back to see me."

A few days later they attended their second interview, this time without Elizabeth. They both sat down in front of the Commander feeling very nervous with dry mouths, short of breath and very worried, wondering to themselves whether she would get a place.

Taking his time as he looked down at his notes, the Commander said, "I have assessed the standard of your daughter's education and I find that she is nearly two years behind my children of the same age." *Oh my God, she hasn't got in*, thought Mavis.

"However," he continued after a suitable pause, "I am prepared to take her, but she will find it very hard for the first two years to catch up."

# Chapter 29

# New Office and New Conventions

With the help of Joan, Barry would spend time in the mornings completing applications and fact finds. Barry's businesses were growing and due to the number of records kept, space was at a premium. Dual Services was expanding as Barry would ask prospective clients if they had insurance and assurance in areas that Hambro Life did not offer.

Joan was now becoming more involved in the business and attended the occasional meeting in the Maidstone office. They had a long discussion as to whether to purchase or rent an office in or around the Medway towns. Barry found a three-storey, freehold building in Rochester High Street which was up for sale. Making an appointment to view, he took Joan with him.

The red brick building, when viewed from the war memorial on the other side of the street, looked like an old Dutch house. It was built well before the Dutch invaded Chatham Dockyard and the Medway, burning the ships of the Royal Navy, in 1667.

The building was owned by three men who ran an import company and comprised of two main floors, attic rooms and a large cellar, each having a toilet and small washroom. On the back wall of the cellar was a bricked-up arch which would originally have been where rowing boats were pulled up from the marshes. On viewing, some of the rooms were full of ladies underwear and shoes. Joan came away with a few pairs of knickers given to her by one of the three partners. Barry thought he fancied her!

After making his calculations, which included renting out the attic, the ground floor and the cellar, Barry decided to purchase the property.

Hambro Life was being sold and the new company, Allied Dunbar, made the existing associates partners enabling them to build up their practices which they could then sell at any time in the future and/or take out loans to be repaid from their practice value. In a few years, Barry's practice was projected to be worth over £1 million.

Barry had opened a bank account for Dual Services at a Barclays Bank branch in Larkfield where he could stop on his way home from the Maidstone office. As he did with all the professionals, Barry made a point of getting to know the Managers as they could be useful to his clients and may pass business over to him if the bank could not help them.

Elizabeth was taking an interest in music, playing the clarinet, and joined the Medway Music Centre. Having private lessons, she progressed quickly and soon joined the Wind Band and the Orchestra. The Centre was always short of money to buy instruments to lend to pupils, so Barry and Mavis decided to hold a barbeque around the swimming pool in their back garden to raise funds. Parents, neighbours, friends and relatives and some of Barry's business contacts were invited.

All went very well and as the drink flowed tongues loosened. The Barclays Bank Manager turned to Barry, drink in hand and slightly slurring his words, as he looked around the garden and swimming pool, "So, this is where some of the bank's money has gone." Barry thought this rather odd as he had neither a loan nor an overdraft with Barclays.

The party was in full swing with Mavis's brother, Ralph, wandering around the pool dressed as a Bunny girl in a skin-tight black swim suit, a white pom pom pinned to his backside and two balloons tucked up in front for breasts. Unfortunately, someone had stuck a pin in one, but he wasn't deflated, he just carried on serving! Just as he turned to go around the pool, one of the Solicitors did a belly flop into the pool and soaked everyone sitting nearby.

On the following Monday Barry said to Joan, "As we are going to move the office to Rochester, can you phone one of the closest of Midland or Lloyds Banks and get me an appointment with the manager? If I like the person, we will transfer the Dual Services account to them."

A few days later Barry met the local Midland Bank Manager.

"Good morning, I have an appointment with the Manager."

"He won't be a moment, Sir," said the young lady at the counter.

The door to the Manager's office opened a minute or two later and the Manager came out. He was of medium height, wearing a grey suit and as he put his hand out Barry noticed the sleeves of his jacket were too long. The Manager's slight smile and expression gave away his thoughts; *I wonder how much he wants to borrow?*

Seated in front of his desk the Manager said, "How can the Bank help?"

"Well, I wish to open an account and I have the last few statements here of Dual Services, it will give you an idea of the transactions."

Barry passed over the statements and observed the Manager's face. His eyes widened and his attitude immediately changed. "Welcome to the Midland," he said.

There was £200,000 in the account!

It was 1976 and Mavis agreed they could go to the two conventions in the USA, but she would only go if Elizabeth could come too and only if they could travel by sea. Barry contacted the convention department of Hambro Life, and it was agreed that as Barry and his family would not be flying, the company would contribute £400 towards the cost.

The two events were to be held on the west coast of America in Los Angeles and San Francisco and with their ship, the QE2, docking in New York, Barry's family would have to travel across the whole of the USA. Mavis said she would also like to meet her pen pal in Canada to whom she had been writing since she was six years old, over thirty-six years.

After a lot of planning, it was decided they would travel First Class on the QE2 to the States and Transatlantic Class coming back, spending around a month in Canada and the USA.

Ten-year-old Elizabeth became friendly with an American girl of about the same age while on board the ship and Mavis and Barry became friendly with the girl's parents. He was an Eye Surgeon and they had been on holiday in the UK. Before going home, they were finishing their vacation in a large, detached house overlooking the sea at Newport, Rhode Island.

"We will be spending just over a month there. Why don't you come and stay with us?"

"That's very kind of you. Perhaps we could come and stay on our way back to the ship, towards the end of our holiday?"

"That will be great, you'll like the house; it's the Secretary of State's summer home and it has some connection to your Royal history."

"Oh, why's that?"

"It's where the Duke of Windsor had an affair with Wallace Simpson!"

Before they left Southampton, Barry had booked a rental car in New York in order to drive to Canada. When the ship was close to New York it was possible to make telephone calls and the Eye Surgeon made a call to book a car. While he was calling, Barry asked him to check his own booking. The car hire firm replied that they did not have a car booked in his name. Barry immediately placed a new booking!

Travelling up New York State towards the Canadian border, a car with two girls went flying by and at almost the same time they could hear a helicopter flying overhead. Then another car raced by. Two to three miles further on there was the first car at the side of the road with the girls surrounded by the Police.

Barry and Mavis started to look for a place to stay for the night. Looking at the map Mavis said, "Shall we try to stay in Rochester; it's only just off the main road?" They called at three hotels, but all were full and one commented that they would be lucky to find a room as there were graduation parties on in the area.

Moving on they found a room in Batavia. They had their first experience of staying in an American hotel: metal doors with three locks!

Being a Friday, the family were told, it was fish night. Having ordered, the waitress told them to help themselves to the bread, pointing to a large table in the centre of the dining room. They were starving! There were three large loaves and the family started to slice off large chunks of the new bread and spread with butter. Big mistake! When the fish came there were three very large chunks of fried fish piled on top of masses of chips. Breakfast was also an experience: eggs in every way possible, pancakes and loads of other items. Looking around at the other guests, they all seemed to be pouring maple syrup on top of everything!

Barry, Mavis, and Elizabeth spent a week in and around Toronto having at last met Barbra, Mavis's pen pal, who she had been writing to since she was six years old. Time came to leave as they had to get to Chicago to catch the train to Los Angeles. They had been driving for some time along the Queen Elizabeth highway when the car began to slow.

"Why are you slowing down?" said Mavis.

"I don't know, it's the car," replied Barry, as he changed to a lower gear without success.

Pulling into the side, the car came to a stop. Having got out and lifted the bonnet, Barry could not see what the problem was. He looked up and down the road to check if there were any emergency phones, in order to ring for help, but there were none. The road was empty, not a car in sight and then, as if God had taken a hand, a lone truck came along! It stopped and two road workers got out.

"What's the problem?" asked one in a broad Canadian accent.

"I don't know, it just would not drive even though the engine is running."

One of them immediately slid down on to his back and began to crawl under the car. He was upright within a few seconds. "The oil has leaked out of the gearbox."

"What can I do, there's no garage and I can't get there any way?"

"Don't worry, we will go and get some oil which may get you to Kent Police Station."

Barry gave them some money in order to buy a can of oil, hoping they would come back. Mavis started to flap! "We've got to get to Chicago to catch the train. How long will they be?"

"Stop worrying," said Barry, "they will be back soon."

In twenty minutes, they were back and proceeded to fill the gear box.

"Thanks very much, fellows, how much do I owe you?" asked Barry.

"You don't owe us anything."

"But what about your fuel?"

"We work on the Highways, so we don't have to pay!"

Barry put his head into the car and came out with a paper bag and said, "Here, have these oranges, we can't take them across the border."

"Thanks, remember what we said, watch for the sign to Kent Police Station and phone Avis and they will come out with another car."

The car began to limp in the gears just as they drove into the Police Station car park; the worry lines started to disappear from Barry's face as he let out a sigh and began to relax. Having explained to the Police he rang from the public phone to London Ontario for ages but no reply so he tried Detroit who said they would send a replacement car.

Some hours later, Mavis having kept on and on that they would miss the train from Chicago, two very tall fit-coloured chaps turned up with another car. On the Queen Elizabeth Highway heading towards the USA and Chicago, Mavis started to worry again. "We'll never make it, the train will have gone by the time we get there."

"Stop worrying, we are gaining two hours."

"What do you mean, gaining two hours?"

"We're going through two time zones heading west!"

The family eventually reached the outskirts of Chicago, without a map, and with no idea as to where Grand Central Station was. Barry kept driving and they found themselves on a hill overlooking Lake Michigan where they parked behind a yellow cab. Getting out, Barry approached the cab driver. "Excuse me, if I pay the fare can I follow you to Grand Central Station?"

"You Australian?"

"No, English."

"Sure, man," said the very large, coloured lady cab driver.

Barry followed the yellow cab in and out of various streets when the driver suddenly turned left down an underground slip road. At the bottom she turned around an island and stopped. Paying the fare, Barry looked at his watch. "Quick, Mavis, the train leaves in ten minutes."

At that moment a Red Cap porter arrived. "Just the man," said Barry, quickly telling him the train they were due to catch, "and I don't have time to return the car," explaining the problems they had with cars.

"Just leave the key under the sun visor, lock the doors and phone the car rental company," the porter said in an Irish accent. He pointed out the phones and Barry contacted the operator for the Avis number.

"What party are you calling?" said the operator in a broad American accent.

"What party? Avis," said Barry in a slightly louder voice as he was getting more and more frustrated.

"Hurry up the train will be leaving," said Mavis from the side.

"What party?"

"**A** for apple, **V** for Victor, **I** for IDIOT and **S** for sugar."

"You don't have to be rude, you mean A'R'VIS?"

Barry phoned the car rental company and told them he had left the car. "You can't do that," came the reply.

"Well, I would not have to do that if your cars didn't break down, and we are not going to miss the train," and he put the phone down.

They all dashed off behind the porter in the hopes of catching the train only to find that the train was running four hours late!

Their sleeping compartments were adjoining, Elizabeth having her own with a door between. The train also had an observation car and Elizabeth soon made friends with the black steward who serviced the car. He would point out the sites and answer her questions and they would chat away. Barry wondered if he just liked listening to her accent.

The train stopped at Albuquerque, and everyone was asked to get off as the staff cleaned the inside while it went through a washing machine to clean the outside. Albuquerque was one of the rare stations which had raised platforms so the passengers could look over a low wall. As they waited, they could see over the car park.

Barry started chatting to the chap standing next to him who said, "I was nearly mugged just now."

"What happened?"

"I went into the station bathroom to have a leak and as I turned to leave a big man stood in front of the door. He pointed a knife at me and said, 'Give me your money.' I was shaking like a leaf, trying to think. I put my hands in my pockets and pulled out all my coins. I said that my money was on the train, this is all I have on me. I threw it in his hand and walked past him, through the door. Any moment I was expecting a knife in my back. As I walked out there were two men in suits, just outside, and I noticed a gold star on one showing under his jacket. I told the Sheriff what had happened and left it to them."

Suddenly there was a loud shout! Both Barry and the guy who had told him the story, looked behind across the low wall and down towards the large car park. They were in time to see a lady ducking her head, about to get in a car – half in, half out – having her bag snatched by a man who ran past, followed by two men in suits running like mad after him.

The man next to Barry, having seen the bag snatch, turned to him and said, "The Police will get on at the next stop to ask me questions."

On arrival in Los Angeles, Barry, Mavis and Elizabeth checked into their room at the Century Plaza Hotel, Century City, with their seven suitcases and started to unpack. Barry's thoughts turned to money. He had purchased two separate lots of American Express cheques, thinking that the first lot would be enough. Opening his wallet and personal bag he could only find one pack.

"What's wrong," said Mavis, breaking off from her unpacking.

"I had two lots of American Express traveller's cheques and I can only find one."

"Oh my God, what are we going to do?" said Mavis in her usual flap, almost flying around the room.

"Don't worry, I'll phone them."

Barry phoned Amex in New York and they gave instructions to call in person at their office in Century City where replacement traveller's cheques could be collected. Little did he know that nearly two years later a letter would arrive at home from American Express informing him that the lost cheques had been handed in but that he had under-claimed... and enclosing a cheque for over £300!

Leaving Los Angeles a week later in a hire car, they made their way to San Francisco in very hot, dry weather. The air conditioning was set at maximum as Barry got out the road maps in order to follow the coast road. They had been travelling for over an hour and the inside of the car was getting hotter and hotter.

"There must be something wrong with the air conditioning, I'm boiling," said Mavis as Elizabeth opened a window and put her bare feet out to catch the breeze as the car travelled along. "You're right, I'll pull in at the next café and have a look."

So much for maps, they were blocking their vents on the front dashboard!

They were due to stay at a Holiday Inn in San Francisco for the next convention. Barry, however, was unaware there was more than one Holiday Inn. Having driven to two, one of which was in Oakland, he asked a receptionist to phone the last hotel to check if the convention was being held there.

Having found it at last, just up from Fisherman's Wharf, they dropped off their luggage, returned the car and settled into their room. The room was large and on the desk were all the usual details of the hotel's services together with a large folder addressed to Barry containing the details of the week's events. In the front it said, 'Please attend the Welcome Reception' in a named meeting room. Mavis and Barry arrived in the room to find it was empty save for a barman. "Do come in, you are the first to arrive,

I believe their plane has been delayed. What can I get you to drink?"

"Thanks, I'll have a gin and tonic." The barman took down a large glass tumbler and started to fill it with ice and Barry, not taking a lot of notice, watched him add a slice of lemon as he turned and poured in the gin and tonic. *Bloody hell*, he thought, *this is strong*. One drink later he went back to their room and was as sick as a dog.

The Convention over, they took a taxi across the bay to Oakland to catch the train to Chicago where they were due to board a plane to Boston. Waiting at O'Hare Airport in Chicago, surrounded by seven suitcases and one large bag containing quality prizes (Elizabeth had helped the caller at bingo by taking out the balls) Mavis said, almost shaking, "I don't want to get on that plane I'm scared. How long is it going to take to get to Boston?"

"I don't know, about two hours I think," Barry replied.

Mavis looked very upset while Elizabeth was looking around, interested in the activity in the airport.

Barry called her back, "Keep Mum company for a minute, Elizabeth."

"Where are you going?" asked Mavis.

"I'm going to see if I can find a Doctor to see if he can give you anything to help you."

Not only was Barry going to try and find a First Aid Station, he also had to find the phones to try and book a hotel in Boston as soon as they landed. Having found the phones, he tried five hotels, but all were full. Time was ticking and they were to catch the last flight, crossing two time zones going east. He could not leave Mavis any longer so he decided to take pot luck and hope he could find a hotel on landing.

"Where have you been?"

"Sorry, I had trouble finding a First Aid post, but the good news is that I have got you a tablet to take."

While Elizabeth looked out the window of the plane at Chicago, Mavis sat as stiff as a rock next to Barry, gripping his hand and starting to draw blood with her fingernails digging into the back of his right hand!

Finally, they landed at an almost empty airport, collected their luggage and stacked the bags on to trolleys. As they walked through the exit Barry looked around for a phone. There on one wall were seven free phones all provided by hotels. Turning to Mavis he said, "Just a minute," and before she could answer he had picked up the first phone. They had two rooms! "We will collect you in fifteen minutes."

"How will I recognise you?"

"You will."

A people carrier with vertical bright red and white strips with 'Ramada Hotel' in very large letters on the side pulled up. It was nearly 1am and they were the last passengers to leave the airport that night.

"I don't suppose the restaurant is still open," said Barry.

"No, but there's an all-night diner across the road," the driver said as he pulled up in the front of the hotel.

Barry turned his head and looked across the road. The diner was less than three minutes' walk away and he said to the driver, "We will walk over there after we have checked in."

The driver looked very surprised, "You can't walk over there; I'll pick you up in twenty minutes."

Next day they picked up another hire car for their journey to Newport, Rhode Island, to stay with the Eye Surgeon and his family they had met on the QE2 coming over to the USA. They stayed at a lovely wooden house overlooking the bay.

The weather was kind and the Surgeon's wife took them to buy live lobsters and crab from an old tin warehouse. She took a very large, strong, black plastic bag and as they entered the warehouse on the left-hand side, they saw large, waist high tanks. The tanks were full of water. Barry looked in the tanks and saw large lobsters with their claws taped up walking along the bottom. A man with a fishing net said, "How many would you like?"

"We would like five lobsters and six crabs, please," said the Surgeon's wife as she opened the large plastic bag and pointed to the ones she wanted.

Having collected their dinner, she took them all around Newport pointing out the massive Rothschild and Vanderbilt houses some of which were then empty. While she drove, there was a noise emanating from the black plastic bag, as the lobsters and crab tried to fight, even though their claws were taped up.

Back at the house, their host asked Barry if he would help her lift a very large and heavy cast iron pot on to the stove. Having filled the pot with water to boil, she chucked in the lobsters and crab and within fifteen minutes the pot was singing as it boiled. She said, "It's not the shell fish making the noise; it's the air being released from their shells." They sat outside on the porch with their tools, eating and looking out across the bay.

Next day they were off in the car to New York to catch the QE2 back to the UK.

Having found on the map the nearest car return office to the QE2 dock, they started to drive through a very run-down area, trying to find the dropping off point. They were hoping there would be a courtesy bus to the ship once they had returned the car. Barry looked around for somewhere to stop. The streets were dirty and some of the buildings looked very run down.

Having parked and locked the car, with Mavis and Elizabeth still in it, he called in the office. "I'm returning a car. Have you a bus to take us to the QE2 pier?"

"No, you will have to call a cab." Barry felt they were not being helpful and as he turned and walked out of the door he was fuming.

Back at the car Barry told Mavis what had transpired and that they were going straight to the pier.

Pulling into the drop-down point at the pier entrance, Barry started to unload the cases as Mavis looked around for a porter. "Hurry up, the ship has almost finished loading, it's due to leave in a minute," said Mavis.

"OK, OK! Give me a chance!"

Barry pushed the door knob to lock the car, shut the door and began to walk away as he checked his back pocket for his wallet. "Shit!"

"What's wrong?"

"I can't find my wallet." Barry's face was creased with worry as he started to trace his steps back towards the car, looking along the ground. He looked in the driver's side window and there on the seat of the locked car was his wallet.

"Now, what are we going to do?" said Mavis in a trembling voice, looking very worried.

Barry turned to see a phone on the wall. He picked up the handset and dialled the hire company.

"We can't get someone out to you; you will have to stop a black and white."

Having overheard, Mavis said, "What's a black and white?"

"A police car."

"But we can't wait, the ship will be sailing soon."

Barry ignored her as he looked across the street, hoping to find a police car. There was not a car in sight. Just before he almost broke out in anger, at that moment a policeman came around the corner. He looked at Barry and then at Mavis who was red with anger and said in a New York accent, "What's the problem?"

Having told the policeman, he turned to Barry and said, "Let's go to the next pier and see if the Pier Master can help."

Barry waited outside for a minute or two while the policeman spoke to the Pier Master who came back waving a wire coat hanger. As he walked to the car, he started to pull the hanger apart and twisted one end into a hook. Reaching the car, he forced the hook behind the glass of the driver's window and placed the hook over the internal door knob and pulled. Click! The door opened.

Having thanked the policeman for his help, Barry looked in his wallet to give him a tip, but the smallest note was $100. "We were always under the impression that you New York coppers were not very helpful. We will go back and tell everyone how helpful you really are. Where do you come from?"

"New Jersey."

# Chapter 30

# QE2

Their cabins were one deck lower than the trip out but seemed identical. Part of the deck they were on could be First Class and part top Trans-Atlantic Class. The dividing cabins would be based on the bookings. As they were familiar with the layout of the ship, they used all the First-Class facilities with the exception of the restaurant. They also discovered the QE2 had two full crews and the current crew was the same one that was on board on the way over.

Their favourite bar was the Midshipmen's, and on the way out to the USA Barry always dressed in his DJ for dinner, with Mavis and Elizabeth in their best long dresses. They would have one or two drinks in the bar before going in for dinner.

On arrival on the first evening the staff greeted them like lost friends. Elizabeth would like to sit at the bar on one of the high stools. They had just sat down when Robbie, who served the tables, approached and addressed them by their surname. "Mrs MacLauchlan would like to be introduced to you. Mrs MacLauchlan is sitting at her table; may I take you over and introduce you?"

Introduction made, Mrs MacLauchlan said, "Please call me Mrs Mac."

Having shaken hands, Mrs Mac said, "Champagne?"

"Yes please," said Mavis.

"Not for me," said Barry, "may I have a gin and tonic?"

Mrs Mac smiled at Elizabeth, "Would you like a Shirley Temple?"

It was the beginning of a very long friendship which was to last many years. Mrs Mac, the youngest daughter of a very wealthy importer from Liverpool, had two sisters who had moved to New York before World War II. Their father had set up a trust fund for all three of them. Mrs Mac, who was one of the first women to go to Liverpool University, had stayed in England during the war. According to her father, she had married beneath her when she married a Wing Commander who died a few years after the war. None of the sisters had children and after Mrs Mac's husband's death, having at last inherited her part of the trust, which was around eight million pounds, she travelled to the USA on the QE2 once a year to stay for six months with her sisters.

Every day Mavis, Elizabeth, and Barry would meet up in the Midshipmen's bar with Mrs Mac and they would drink a bottle, or more, of Moet Champagne. As a regular passenger Mrs Mac was well known and would receive visitors to her table, many of whom were on the make trying to tap her up to invest in various schemes. One day two gay Americans in their late thirties tried to get her to invest in real estate but Mrs Mac politely refused.

A surgeon from Southampton was returning from a lecture in New York in which he demonstrated his new operation with a pickled leg. He was invited to have a drink and started to tell of the problems of getting a pickled leg through the US Customs!

Mrs Mac always dressed in light coloured pant suits which seemed to match the colour of her hair. She explained to Mavis that she had a number of scars on her legs due to horse riding accidents.

"Excuse me, my dear, I must go to the loo," said Mrs Mac as she got up from her chair. Some minutes later she returned in a flustered state, almost running, gripping the side of her white pants.

"I have got the zip stuck."

"Here, let me try," said Mavis.

"Don't worry about that; have you a pair of scissors?"

"But you will ruin your pants!"

"I'll buy a new pair. Anyway, I've more suits in my cabin."

"I've a pair of scissors in our cabin," said Mavis.

"Let's run down and you can cut it out," said Mrs Mac.

"But we haven't finished our Champagne!"

"Wash your hair in it, take it with us."

That was a sight to behold: two ladies running along the deck, one holding a champagne bottle, the other with white/silver hair in a matching suit, chasing behind holding her pants up with her right hand and her evening shoes in the other and shouting, "Cut the bloody thing, I'm bursting to go to the loo."

Barry was talking to two of the bar tenders. "Mavis has seen a ring she likes in one of the shops; she keeps going on about it. If I bought it, do you think I should declare it at Customs?"

"No, you should be alright, don't bother."

On arrival at Southampton the passengers' luggage was laid out in a warehouse in alphabetical order. Barry, Mavis, and Elizabeth walked to section 'W' and went to collect their luggage. Mavis was carrying her coat over her arm when a Customs officer approached them.

"Have you anything to declare, Sir?"

"No."

"Have you anything to declare, Madam?"

"No."

Mavis was looking down at the concrete floor, not making eye contact with the Customs officer. They both appeared nervous. He asked the question again to both of them and the response was the same. All around them passengers and porters were picking up luggage and making their way to the exits. Most were catching the boat train to London.

"Come with me, please," said the Customs officer as he walked towards an office. "Sit down," he said in a stern voice. As they sat at a metal desk the officer walked out and Barry and Mavis were left alone in the office with no windows, white walls, a blank desk and just one chair on the other side. They were too frightened to say anything and just looked at each other with very worried faces.

Two men in uniform walked in, one of whom had a sheet of paper in his hand and said, "I am charging you both under (quoting some act)," but by now, Mavis and Barry were not listening as they thought to themselves how stupid they had been.

"You will pay the duty due and a fine. We have your names on file, and should you again try to evade customs duty within the next two years you may face a prison sentence. We will confiscate the ring and if you wish you can pay by credit card, now. You can then pick up the ring in two months' time."

Shaking, carrying their luggage, Barry and Mavis came out of the warehouse to find the train to London had gone and they were the only people on the platform, having just paid out over £1,800.

# Chapter 31

# Another Business

The following year Barry decided to have the garden landscaped and after interviewing a number of contractors, he chose a chap from Rochester. After giving him instructions, Barry left him alone to get on with the job but checked progress daily in the late afternoon.

Arriving home early one day the landscaper was still in the garden and Barry took him a cup of coffee. They got chatting over their drinks. "This is a lovely house," said the landscaper looking up at the three storeys from where he was standing in the garden. "What do you do to be able to afford a house like this?"

"Well, I'm in Financial Services and I also have a small management consultancy."

"What does the consultancy do?"

"We look at companies who are in trouble, need finance, or need improvements in the way they are run and prepare a report for which we charge a small fee. In our recommendations we may also introduce other professionals such as accountants, solicitors, and banks or other lenders and investors."

"Would you be prepared to look at my business?"

"Of course."

A week or so later Barry went to have a look at the landscaper's place of business. It was on the outskirts of Rochester in an area of land amongst houses with the entrance between a bungalow and a house. The area spread behind the bungalow and was around three quarters of an acre. Two old sheds attached to each other were used as a shop selling produce growing on the site together with gardening items. The land was owned by the landscaper and his wife, except for a 'ransom strip' down one side.

Having prepared the report, they all met at Barry's house to discuss it and the outcome was a legal partnership. Barry would inject funds and deal with the bank. Joan and the landscaper would invoice the landscaping jobs and pay creditors with Joan dealing with the bookkeeping. The landscaper and his wife also had a lease on a large greenhouse not far from Tenterden which they ran as a Garden Centre, but this business was not made part of the partnership.

Barry and Joan moved into the offices in Rochester High Street with the aid of a draw down from his practice value and a bank bridging loan. Barry then proceeded to arrange a 10-year mortgage to repay the bank.

Barry was now working even longer hours, visiting clients and prospective clients. Solicitors, banks and accountants would recommend him to their clients. This became a two-way business with their practices receiving new referrals from Barry.

A solicitor with a practice in Maidstone, who became a client, referred him on to an ex-member of the Kent Police. Having booked an appointment, Barry called to see him some two weeks later. On the first visit, collecting the information for the report, Barry asked him if he could think of other people who might be interested in his services.

"I don't know if you would be prepared to see him, but there is a chap I nicked while in the force. I and a few others thought him a likeable rogue. He lives in West Kingsdown. We had had a tip off that some whisky had been stolen and suspected this chap, Kenny Noye, might have been involved.

"Four of us turned up at his house, a small bungalow, and I sent two of the officers next door to make their way around the back. Having pressed the doorbell and waiting for what seemed like ages, the door was slowly opened by his wife. She was one of the most beautiful women I had ever seen, wearing hot pants her golden-brown legs seem to go up to her arm pits! She was wearing a low-cut blouse and leaned against the side of the door and started to chat to us in a silky, sexy voice.

"Being men, we were enjoying looking and flirting until I realised she was keeping us at the door giving Kenny a chance to get away! Meanwhile, Kenny was lifting cases of whisky over the back fence! Having nicked him, we took him to our cop shop and charged him. The interview, which lasted a few hours, did not produce much and we were about to have a break when Kenny said, 'Any chance someone could look at my foot, I think I've broken it?' It turned out he had been sitting there in massive pain for all those hours and not said a word!"

It took a few weeks for Barry to get an appointment. Arriving at his house on the edge of a small estate, Barry rang the doorbell and was greeted by Kenny's extremely attractive wife. He was shown into the lounge and over coffee with them both Barry completed his fact find to return a week later.

A year or so later Barry called on another solicitor in Swanley at the only other practice in the town who was already his client and had recommended him to some of his clients including his sister. He got chatting to Brian, the new solicitor, and when writing down his home address he mentioned that Kenny Noye lived in the same road. Brian said, "I live opposite." The conversation then turned to Kenny's antics.

"You know about the Rolls Royce?"

"No, I didn't know he had one." Barry thought to himself, *I had better give him a service call.*

"He came out of his house one morning, looked at the car and went mad. During the night someone had scratched all down one side and thrown paint over the other side."

Calling on another legal practice in Maidstone, Barry discovered that they had represented Kenny for his early court cases.

"Hello, Ken, just calling to see how you are and to arrange a service call to update my records."

"I'm not bad, when do you want to come?"

Having arranged the meeting, Barry turned up at Kenny's House to be greeted by his wife. "Ken is not here, he is round at the yard."

Having never been there before, Barry asked for directions. The yard turned out to be a high wire fenced compound with a large warehouse. Within the concrete yard was a green Portacabin alongside the warehouse. The gate was open, and he parked near the cabin. Kenny invited Barry in. "How are things, Ken?"

"Bloody coppers, they raided the yard the other day, accused me of receiving, the bastards!"

"Why? What happened then?"

"One of my mates phoned and said that a couple of his blokes need to stop off in their lorries because of exceeding their hours. It's this new tachograph. He asked if they could park up in the yard and I said it would be okay. They turned up about two hours later, dropped off their trailers, left them in the yard and drove off. About ten minutes later all hell let loose, the place was surrounded by coppers in their cars. The trailers had been nicked and I am being done for receiving!"

That was the last time Barry met Kenny. He had called around to the house and his wife said he was in the USA looking at importing large American caravans. He called again a couple of months later, but he had moved without leaving a forwarding address. The last time Barry checked he was still in receipt of his commission.

A referral from a solicitor took Barry to an optician. He was an Iranian, his wife being German and heavily pregnant. During the fact find Barry found that they wished to purchase a disused school and convert it into a family home. They needed a loan or mortgage to cover the cost. He also discovered that they had no life cover or pensions and said that he would try and obtain an offer of a loan. On his return two weeks later, Barry reported that he was having difficulty in obtaining finance for the school purchase, but he would continue to do his best to obtain funds. This took place in the mid to late 1970s.

# Chapter 32

# Mr Rochester

The 1980s were exciting years for Barry with the growth in the businesses, lots of travel and invitations, so much so that some events had to be turned down due to lack of time and Mavis being afraid of flying!

The family had started to learn to ski in the winter of 1979/80 and, although hard work, found it great fun. Their instructor was an English girl of about 20. Her name was Elizabeth (Liz), the same name as Barry's daughter. She was slim, blond with blue eyes and very beautiful with a lovely soft voice. Lined up across a snow-covered slope, looking like birds on a wire, the instructor demonstrated to the beginners how to do the snow plough. She then stood on her skis with her legs apart and the inside edges turned inwards in a v shape to stop herself from sliding down the hill. She then turned her skis flat and parallel to each other and started to go down the slope, stopping by repeating the snow plough.

Barry was standing third in line from the top with a couple alongside at the beginning of the line. They all had to try the snow plough in front of the class. A rather big lady went off first, like a bat out of hell, bending forward and looking like a gorilla on skis SCREAMING, "I can't stop!" She ended up head first in a snow drift, her backside up in the air with her legs apart and her husband shouting: "Not now, dear, not in front of all these people."

The city of Rochester promoted a number of festivals throughout each year, including Dickens, Sweeps, Jack in the Green and more. An article in the local paper mentioned that there was to be a competition to find a Mr Rochester. Without telling him, Mavis and Elizabeth decided to enter Barry dressed in a Victorian bathing costume which they would knit in wool. The rules for the competition stated that no artificial aids were to be worn under any costume. The big day came, and Barry could be seen being almost dragged down the High Street by two laughing ladies in Dickensian costumes towards the Royal Victoria and Bull Hotel.

"But what am I to wear?" said Barry laughing. *I can't wear this*, as he looked down at his Dickensian attire. He was wearing a very long, pale grey almost blue, great coat, black trousers tucked into red/brown riding boots in East Kent Hunt colours.

"We have got your costume in here," said Mavis pointing to the bag.

They went into the hotel and registered, giving Barry's name and other details. They were shown to a bedroom in which he could change. "Now, we will wait downstairs while you change. But remember you are not to wear your underpants or anything else under the costume."

Barry opened the bag and held up the contents. It was a woollen knitted bathing costume in bright green and yellow horizontal stripes with sleeves almost down to his elbows and the legs coming down to the top of his knees.

Having changed, he put on his high-top hat and boots, leaving his socks off, and went down the stairs to meet Mavis and Elizabeth. Standing in the Reception area were seven other gentlemen, all in different costumes. One chap was dressed as a chimney sweep. He had white long johns down to his ankles with a white vest covering his arms, all in wool. Over his shoulder he held a sweep's brush with a dirty black bag attached. His face was black with soot as were his hands.

"Gentlemen, will you all take your shoes off and leave them along that side wall," the lady said pointing to a wall away from the Reception. Will you please follow me in single file down the High Street and then up into the Castle grounds and on to the Band Stand."

In bare feet, they all followed the lady at a brisk pace down the High Street. Out in front a Dickensian dressed man kept shouting, "Make way for the Mr Rochester competitors; see them in the Castle Gardens," as the clapping crowds parted.

The festival was underway with the kids playing on the swings. A large crowd was being entertained while they waited for the Mr Rochester competition to start. The competitors were introduced over the Tannoy to the assembled crowd. They were asked to flex their muscles and answer silly questions, the crowd laughing, clapping and having a good time. What Barry had not seen was state of his costume between his legs. The three judges would have noticed the green and yellow stripes sagging down giving the impression of him having rather large genitalia! The winner was announced, BARRY, the first Mr Rochester! The year was 1981. Carrying a page three girl – unfortunately she was not topless – around the Castle grounds, Barry noticed a number of ladies looking down between his legs and he wondered why.

In the same year Barry joined the Rotary Club of Rochester.

Always seeking to increase his client list, Barry designed a new seminar format which he hoped would encourage more business and professional people to attend. He decided to hold them on board the Olau Line ferry which sailed at 10am on a Monday from Sheerness in Kent to Vlissingen in the Netherlands, returning the following day. The format included a number of speakers on various subjects including legal, tax, finance and investment, including pensions. Lunch, cabin accommodation and transport into Middelburg would be free for speakers and attendees. These seminars became a great success and were profitable for the speakers as well as Barry's business. On the third year of running these seminars he earned nearly thirty thousand pounds one a single trip.

Barry was becoming known in Rochester; shop keepers, council employees who organised events and professionals would greet him in the street. One day he noticed a 'Flat for Sale' board on the building next to his office. Having looked at the flat he decided to purchase it as an investment.

When he had purchased his office building it included a small area to the rear on which stood a dilapidated building with a small tree growing through it and was almost completely overgrown. Entry to the building was gained through an alleyway sufficiently wide to allow cars access to the council car park. He arranged to have the building demolished, and the area concreted over so that he had two parking places. A few weeks later he received a letter from Medway Council stating that he had concreted over their land and insisting he remove the concrete and reinstate their car park. Barry responded and asked for details of the area in question and proof of ownership. No reply was received.

Some nine months later a gate was erected across the alleyway blocking the entrance to both Barry's parking places and the public car park. Barry removed the gate, stood it up against his office wall and asked Medway Council to collect it. Having checked his deeds once again, Barry established that the owner of his office building had ingress rights. Letters flowed backwards and forward, the gate was replaced and removed; finally, having provided evidence to the Council as to his rights, the gates were never replaced again!

Rather than leaving empty the two floors above his offices, three floors in total plus a basement, Barry decided to let them out. The rental income would also help to pay off the mortgage. He received an enquiry for the National Dock Labour Board to rent the two top floors and the board manager and his secretary, representatives for Chatham Dock Yard, occupied the offices.

Late one evening the manager left in a hurry to attend a meeting at the Dock Yard. Getting into his car he realised he had left a file back in the office. Returning to the office, almost running up the stairs, the manager suddenly stopped. He felt very cold. The stairs, which were in semidarkness, seemed to be moving. He became very frightened and ran! Next day he recounted his experience to Joan, Barry's partner.

By now there were two employees, Joan in her office and Barry in his large office at the front overlooking the High Street. His furniture was highly polished which the cleaning lady would bring up to a high gloss every day.

One morning the cleaning lady said to Joan, "Can you ask Barry not to let his young children play in his office and put their fingers all over his desk?"

"But he does not have any young children," said Joan, "his only daughter is away at Nottingham Polytechnic."

Arriving early one day Barry placed the key in his office door, opened it and there in the centre of the floor was a toy car. It was the size and length of his thumb, an old fashion Harrods truck made of lead and painted in Harrods' colours. Looking around he noticed two of his paintings on the wall were all at an angle. Going to his desk he could see four little fingerprints.

At a dinner party some weeks later, he mentioned the fingerprints and the manager's experience and one of the ladies said, "I was walking from the Cathedral past the War Memorial and for some reason I looked up at the small round window at the top of your building. There was a little girl in a poke bonnet, the type a servant would wear, looking out."

Some years later, after the National Dock Labour Board had ceased to exist following Margaret Thatcher's closure of the scheme, Barry was clearing out the top floor. He removed some panels and on the floor behind them he found an old mattress.

One morning as Barry was preparing recommendations for his clients Joan came into his office and said, "I have two chaps in their late twenties to early thirties who would like to see you."

"I wonder what they want? Best show them in."

Barry stood up to shake their hands as they came through the door. They were about two inches shorter than him, and both were wearing suits. He vaguely recognised them and was trying to place where he had seen them before.

"We came to see you because we understand you are interested in buying property in the High Street."

"Well, I have been looking around," said Barry, "what have you in mind?"

"Our father has entered into a contract to purchase number forty-nine, but he now finds he cannot raise the money. We were wondering if you would like to buy it."

"Who owns it at the moment?"

"Nick the Greek."

"The alcoholic?"

"Yes."

Barry had seen Nick wobbling down the High Street, almost falling over, his clothes half on and half off, shouting in his broken English, with a half-empty bottle of whisky in his hand. People would cross the street to get out of his way. He would go into the sweet shop and try to grope the young lady shop assistants.

The two brothers warned Barry to contact their father about 8am before he started on his first bottle of the day.

On the day Barry called to view the property Nick had only just got out of bed. He looked very rough, hair all over the place, bloodshot eyes and was only half-dressed. The place did not look as if had been cleaned in the last few weeks.

"Why do you want to sell?"

"I want to go back to Greece to die. Don't try to do business with me after eleven in the morning. If I change my mind about selling, take no notice of me, I shall be drunk!"

# Chapter 33

# The Writ

Having purchased the property, Barry obtained quotes to refurbish it into an upmarket coffee shop selling luxury cakes. Mavis and he had got the idea from Austrian coffee shops. A week after the builders had started work, he called in to see the progress and one of the workmen said, "A chap keeps looking in and keeps asking for the owner."

"Next time he calls in tell him to come and see me at my office."

Some days later the man spoke to Joan and said that he had agreed a price, and he was purchasing the property! She told him to make an appointment to see Barry.

Prior to the meeting Barry checked with his solicitor that all was in order who confirmed that the purchase money had indeed been paid and that he was holding the deeds on Barry's behalf.

The gentleman, having presumably contacted his solicitor, did not mention that he owned the property. He asked if he could rent it as he wished to open a restaurant. Barry refused to grant him a lease. Almost every week the man phoned, called in to the property to see the progress and asked the builders what the building was going to be used for. A lady called into Barry's office one day and Barry happened to be available. She was dark haired with an attractive face but just a little too much make up and seemed to be in her mid-fifties.

"Please, can we please have a lease?" Barry relented and granted a ten-year lease.

The office post on most days was opened by Joan, date stamped, sorted and Barry's placed on his desk. But this day Joan came in looking worried and said in a somewhat cracking voice, "A writ has been issued against you."

"What do you mean?"

"Look at this," said Joan and handed over the official looking papers.

Reading through the document he found that the plaintiff was a client of his, an optician, who had asked him to try and obtain a loan to purchase a disused school to convert into a dwelling. At the time Barry could not find any organisations willing to lend. The optician was suing for the return of premiums, pension contributions and damages. Barry phoned his Professional Indemnity Insurers who told him not to respond and to send the documents to them. The case was listed to be heard in Croydon and lasted nearly two years. It was twice thrown out of court by the Judge, telling the plaintiff's brief on the last occasion that if he had to send him back again, he would find for the defendant. Barry did not have to appear in the witness box until the last two occasions.

Barry was in the witness box being cross examined by the plaintiff's brief:

"As a broker…"

"I am not a broker."

The questions continued: "As a broker…"

Barry said again, "I am not a broker."

More questions and then he said again: "As a broker…"

That was it, red rag to a bull. Barry started to give the impression that he was losing his temper. The Judge intervened, addressing the plaintiff's brief: "The defendant has already stated he is not a broker and if you address him like that again I will find for the defendant."

The case continued with questions from the briefs being fired at both parties till they summed up and the Judge retired to reach his verdict. Both parties sat outside for some hours waiting for the court to reconvene. Finally, the usher called them all in to await the Judge and his verdict. Barry's brief said, "Come and sit next to me to hear what the Judge has to say."

The Judge took almost an hour; one moment Barry thinking he had lost, the next thinking he had won. All he could remember was the Judge saying, "I find the defendant to be a very professional gentleman," as he found in Barry's favour!

His brief said, "I wish we could have taped that, it was a brilliant summing up. Come down to the robing room and we can have a chat."

Entering the room the first person to greet Barry was the plaintiff! "I'm sorry," he said, "could you come and see me and review my insurance cover?"

"I will check my diary to see if I can fit it in," said Barry. He never did visit the plaintiff again!

As he was driving home, he started thinking about the case and why the plaintiff had tried to sue him. After a while he remembered him saying, during the fact find at their first meeting, that his brother had a construction business in Persia, and he was part owner. He must have lost the money he had invested when the Shah abdicated, and the country became Iran.

In 1984 Hambro Life changed its name to Allied Hambro and in 1985 it became Allied Dunbar after Dunbar Bank was purchased.

One Friday lunchtime at a Rotary meeting Barry was approached by a fellow Rotarian who said, "Barry, you have an interest in Garden Centres."

"I have a half share in one, why do you ask?"

"A friend of mine has just died leaving a widow and three kids. They live in a house on some acres which has traded as a nursery. She does not have much money and has not run the business, she needs help. Can you go and see her and see if you can help?"

The widow showed Barry around the extensive grounds. There were a number of greenhouses, some empty and others with conifers growing on. Outside there were fields of conifers of different sizes. In other fields there were more shrubs. Some way away set in a pit outside, there was an oil-fired boiler used to heat the greenhouses during the winter. Barry arranged to take his partner from their other garden centre to visit and give him his opinion.

The terms of a lease were agreed with the widow and both parties consulted their solicitors to draw up the agreement. The weeks went by and both Barry and his partner were itching to get started with planting bedding for the new season. They had plans to open the site as a garden centre and needed to convert one of the large greenhouses as a shop. Some of the bedding would be sold to the other two centres at a discount thereby increasing sales and profits. However, time was of the essence. Barry kept pestering his solicitor to finalise the lease who told him that the widow's solicitor was dragging it out.

If they were to be able to grow the plants and indeed look after the existing shrubs in order to have stock to open in time, they had to get on site immediately.

Barry spoke to the widow and agreed a rent. He then phoned his solicitor who advised him not to go ahead but to wait for the lease. However, Barry decided to take a chance, partly to help the lady out financially as she had three young children, and also to take advantage of the coming season.

At first all went well. Staff were taken on and wooden buildings were put in for letting out to others and a teashop with Mavis and Joan helping serving tea and cakes. But after many months there was still no sign of the lease.

Coming into the third year, things started to happen on the site. Tools went missing, equipment was broken, and other items scattered around, as though vandals had spent a night on the site. One morning Barry arrived very early in the hope of catching them. Walking around he could find no trace until by chance he walked up to the boiler house. It was completely burnt out.

Having reported the events to the Police sometime previously, they had not been able to trace anyone, but things could not continue. No lease, fire and other damage. Barry decided it was time to have a closing down sale and move all the stock left to the other centres.

Sometime later he found out that the widow had had a new man in her life.

## Chapter 34

## Broken Fun

In 1989 Mavis and Barry were invited, for the second time, to a winter convention in St Moritz. They set of in the Jaguar fully loaded with ski gear, suitcases and daughter Elizabeth (for whom they had paid £400 per night for room only on one of the lower floors of the Klum Hotel), five bags, skis and skiwear.

The weather in England was overcast with a slight drizzle as they boarded the hovercraft to France. Barry drove off the beach in Calais and was surprised to find that in the shady areas the road was covered in ice with the surrounding trees covered in frost on his shortcut to Dunkirk.

Barry joined six other cars, stuck behind a small British registered car travelling at no more than 20 miles per hour. As the road began to straighten out in the sunshine, the cars began to overtake. It came to Barry's turn. He accelerated and passed just as he came to a shady part of the road. The car went out of control, sliding across the ice, his daughter screaming, "DAD!" *CRASH!*

The car had hit a concrete electricity pole which was slowly falling towards the car. "DAD GET OUT!" shouted Elizabeth as she pulled him out of the passenger side. The pole missed the driver's side by three or four inches as it crashed down. They stood there trying to avoid the cables which were sparking and crackling as they did a merry dance across the ice.

The ambulance was called and Elizabeth, who spoke French, went with Mavis to Calais Hospital. Barry stayed waiting for the car to be collected on a low loader. After a long wait the car and Barry arrived at a garage which was about to shut for lunch. Speaking broken English and using hand gestures, he was later deposited at a house and offered coffee. Barry asked if he could make phone calls to the insurers in the UK regarding his car and to arrange a hired car to drive on to Austria.

Some three hours and many phone calls later a taxi took Barry to the ferry terminal. Asking the taxi driver to wait, Barry went in to the terminal expecting to see the hire car desk open, as he had been told. It was closed. Back to the taxi, "Take me to the Hoverport." It was closed! Back again to the ferry terminal.

The taxi driver was starting to get annoyed, "Monsieur, I 'ave other people to pick up!"

Just as Barry walked into the ferry terminal, he could see an AA man at his desk. His phone rang, and looking at Barry, he said, "Monsieur, it's for you."

Barry thought to himself, *Who the hell knows I'm here? Could it be the insurers?* He took the phone from the AA man. "Dad, it's me, I'm at the hospital, they have discharged Mum."

"Is she alright?"

"Yes, just a badly bruised arm, they have put it in a sling."

"You have some money, take a taxi to the ferry terminal."

Just as Barry finished the call a rather beautiful tall lady in a red suit came to open up the car hire desk.

"Are you waiting for a car?"

"Yes," said Barry, giving her his name.

Having dealt with the paperwork, the taxi driver and Barry unloaded the cases, ski gear and skis whilst the car hire lady went and collected the hire car. The car seemed to be a lot smaller than the Jag as Barry packed the cases in whilst trying to leave room for Mavis in the back.

Mavis got out of the taxi with Elizabeth and looked around, "There he is, by that car over there. What's he doing?"

"He's loading that car up."

"I thought we were going home," said Mavis to Barry as she stood there with her arm in a sling.

"No, we are going on to our apartment. I've hired this car, and we have a four-wheel drive car to pick up from the garage in Soll. I can drive that over the mountains to St Moritz."

They had leased an apartment two years ago, in Soll near Kufstein, Austria, for ten years. It was a small one-bedroom apartment with a second sleeping area on a mezzanine area off the sitting room.

They arrived in Soll at 3am the next day and after a long sleep, Barry walked to the local garage and picked up the four-wheel drive car ready to load up for the following day.

The road was open. The red and white poles, which indicate whether a road is closed, were up as they drove to Switzerland. Having stayed there before, Barry drove to Badrutts Palace overlooking the lake which at this time of the year was frozen over and used as a horse racing track.

Immediately, he stopped the car they were surrounded by four bell boys who started to unload the luggage. The car was a small two door Suzuki, and the bell boys had the surprise of their lives when they came across Mavis tucked in the back surround by cases! Barry went to reception to check in. "Sorry, Sir, you are not staying here, you are staying at the Klum. Don't worry about your luggage, we will bring it to the Klum, just go and check in and have a nice day."

Barry, Mavis and Elizabeth took the Corviglia Funicular up to the main ski area. They then transferred to the cable car which took them to the top of the mountain. At the top was a small flat area on which to alight and a tiny restaurant and then it was straight down the side to the next lift. The main ski area, around the middle station, comprised of a few chair lifts with a large number of tee bar drag lifts. One particularity long tee bar was so rutted your teeth chatted as you hit every bump.

The day of the Gala Dinner arrived. Barry and Mavis had just finished skiing and Barry carried Mavis's as well as his own skis, one on each shoulder, across the car park. There had not been very much snow in the last few days and the car park was covered in grit.

"Come on hurry up, I've booked to have my hair done for tonight and we will miss the bus!" said Mavis.

Alright, alright I'm coming as fast as..." *CRASH!* Barry went flying and the skis flew everywhere. He put his left arm down to try to save himself. *CRACK!* Nearby was a tall brick wall on the top of which sat skiers drinking at a café and stacked against that wall were their skis. Barry struggled to get up holding his wrist. He felt sick and went and sat with his back to the wall. Suddenly all the skis stacked against the wall fell like a pack of cards. The skiers shouted but one look from Mavis and they all went quiet.

"We had better take you to the hospital."

"No, it might get better soon."

Back at the hotel Mavis had to help Barry get dressed in his DJ as he could not use his left hand. Just as she helped him on with his jacket there was a tap on the bedroom door. Opening the door, there stood a chap with his DJ jacket in his hand. "I'm next door, can you help me I've broken my shoulder, and I can't get my jacket on!"

At dinner Mavis cut up Barry's food and he used his right hand to eat.

Next day, having packed the cases in the car, Elizabeth said as she got in to drive, "Let's find the nearest hospital."

"No," said Barry, "drive to Worgl, it's just down the road from the apartment in Soll."

Mavis and Elizabeth took turns driving the car over the mountain passes to Worgl. On reaching the outskirts of the town they pulled into a garage to ask for directions to the krankenhaus, a lovely word for hospital. On arrival at the krankenhaus, Elizabeth took her father into the accident department where he was seen very quickly.

Elizabeth took Barry into the hospital and having registered they sat down to wait. Within minutes, Barry's name was called, and both looked up to see a slim young lady, no taller than Elizabeth, who was quite short, in a white coat. She rattled away in German, with Barry not understanding a word, to which Elizabeth replied also in German, as the nurse walked away with them following.

"What's happening?" said Barry.

"She's taking you to X-ray."

The two of them sat waiting to see the X-ray results when two white coated men came rushing by pushing a trolley on which lay a man, moaning. His bare leg covered in blood was hanging half off the trolley. Elizabeth's face turned white. She got up off the chair and nearly fell over, turned, and ran out of the hospital!

The young nurse returned holding the X-ray in her hand. She looked for Elizabeth but seeing only Barry she waved her hand to indicate for Barry to follow her. They entered a small alcove which had a frame fixed to a wall into which the nurse placed the X-ray. She switched on the light behind the frame showing up Barry's left wrist. She pointed to it as she said something in German. Barry did not have a clue what she was saying but stared hard at the X-ray. He looked at the area where the nurse pointed. It looked like a hole about the size of a penny just below the joint in his wrist with a crack in the bone just above the hole. Barry at last understood what she was saying. It did not take Barry long to realise that this was what the Doctors at his Army medical kept questioning about his left arm!

As they were studying the X-ray another nurse in a white coat arrived, glanced at it and turned to Barry and said, "Come with me," in broken English. Barry looked up into her beautiful eyes and almost melted on the spot but would have followed her anywhere. They entered another room which had a blue curtain on a brass rail at chest height down the centre of the room. A bed covered in a white sheet was parallel to the curtain. The nurse told Barry to lie down on the bed with his left arm touching the curtain. His mind was going mad day dreaming of this beautiful nurse, *take me anytime.*

Barry lay down and as he did so, he noticed a short vertical stainless-steel rod on a stand, somewhat like a standard lamp. A rod stuck out at right angles with what looked like five springs of different sizes hanging down. The nurse, leaning on his chest, getting him all excited, took hold of his arm below the wrist with one hand and started to insert his fingers into the springs with her other hand. Barry, breathing hard and enjoying every moment and the smell of her perfume, wondered what was going to happen next. The nurse then hung a weight from his upper arm and elbow pulling his arm downwards from his fingers.

From behind the blue curtain came the sound of talking and then suddenly a scream. The curtains moved and parted in the centre as a man's blooded leg could be seen. There were lots of bits of stone sticking out of the leg and he was screaming as one nurse held him down and the other pulled the stones out. Another skiing accident!

On returning to the car, his arm now in plaster, Barry suddenly remembered that he had broken his left arm at the age of eight jumping off an air raid shelter. It must have left the hole as it healed.

# Chapter 35

# Pickwick Club

About two weeks after Barry became Mr Rochester, he received an invitation to a meeting at the Royal Bull and Victoria Hotel to discuss the formation of a Rochester Pickwick Club. The invitations had been sent by a gentleman of the stature of Pickwick: rotund, small feet and of a jovial nature. He mentioned that although there were a number of Pickwick Clubs around the world, sadly none associated with Rochester even though Charles Dickens had lived nearby and based many of his books on the area. He went on to say that Rochester had its Dickens Festival with no Pickwick Club.

At the meeting, all those attending agreed to the formation of such a club and having agreed to the individual names given to them – Weller, Wardle, Jingle, Snodgrass, Tupman and others – set some simple rules. They would all dress in Dickensian costume at functions, including club dinners. When addressing other club members, they would always use their Dickensian name.

Over a period of time the club became well known at festivals around Kent. All the characters dressed in appropriate attire as their name suggested. They came to the notice of Medway Council who started to ask them to represent the city. At the annual Dickens Festival, the Pickwick Club would lead the parade. Sometime after the parade one year, a spectator phoned Barry ("Wardle") to say that his friend in New York had seen the Pickwick Club on TV.

Barry's Allied Dunbar business was doing well with clients and professionals recommending him to their clients. He had been dealing with a medium-sized accountancy practice with five partners who had their offices in Villiers Street, London, alongside Charing Cross Railway Station. Reciprocal business had been going on for some years with three of the partners. One of the owners of a very successful company happened to be at their offices on the same day as Barry and the partner dealing with his account called Barry into his office to introduce him. Having briefly discussed his business, Mr White, the owner, invested a small amount of money from his company into a pension for himself and his wife. The following year Barry persuaded the accountant to give him some details of the company's profit figures. Barry then arranged to visit the client at his offices near Southampton.

Barry arrived at the office just before 10am. The receptionist asked Barry to take a seat and advised him that Mr White would be there shortly. Barry sat there for around minutes before Mr White arrived. "Hello," he said as he walked through the door. "Follow me, we will go to my office."

Mr White was a large man, slightly taller than Barry, with black hair and bushy eyebrows somewhat like Dennis Healy. Barry followed him into his office. Looking around there were two chrome chairs with black leather seats facing his desk. The desk was made of clear glass through which you could see the carpet, no drawers, with just a phone and an ashtray on the top. What surprised Barry was the lack of any paper. On one wall was a large painting of a white yacht under sail in a rough sea of deep blue. Barry commented that it was a lovely painting. "Do you like it? It's my yacht."

The conversation moved to the state of the economy, future projections and taxation. This gave Barry the opening he needed to mention tax savings and directors' future benefits. Having filled his pipe, Mr White puffed away as he listened.

"How much can the company invest for this year?"

Barry explained the maximum figure based on the net profits of the company.

Mr White looked at his watch. "Let's go and have some lunch and I'll give you a cheque on our return. I have my wife's car today," he said as they got into a BMW.

He drove like a bat out of hell, down single-track county lanes, corners at speed and hardly looking as he crossed junctions. Fear showing on his face, Barry gripped the door handle ready to throw himself out! They eventually arrived at the back entrance of a pub where Mr White greeted the landlord and ordered the beers.

"The landlord is one of my crew, so we will have a good meal."

"What will you have, steak?"

"Two steaks and a bottle of the house red."

When they had finished their meal, Mr White suggested they sit up at the bar. Pointing to a bottle of Glenmorangie, which was nearly full, he said, "We will have that whisky bottle on the bar with two glasses."

The two of them finished the bottle and Mr White drove back, just as fast, passing a policeman motorcyclist on the way. As promised, he gave a large cheque to Barry.

Barry poured himself into his car, praying all the way back, and he managed to get home safely. The following year and every November after that, when he visited Mr White, Barry would drive himself there and be driven home by a retired police woman!

Every year there were two overseas conventions: Greece, Cannes, the Caribbean, Monte Carlo and many more. Although invited, Barry and Mavis did not attend due to Mavis's fear of flying. She did, however, agree to attend the conventions in Paris, Vienna and St. Moritz (twice).

After a huge row and lots of crying from Mavis, Barry went on his own to Barbados in 1985 and flew first class to Hong Kong in 1986.

Arriving in Barbados in the evening, about twelve of them boarded a minibus. Barry sat just behind the driver. It soon became clear why there were a number of small buses and not a large coach, the roads were only narrow lanes. Looking around the countryside reminded Barry of the West Country in the 1950s. The black and white striped traffic poles and signs and tin shacks, some used as bars serving drinks and snack food. Suddenly the driver swerved, and Barry could see bodies lying in the road. "Aren't you going to stop?" Barry asked.

"No, it's Friday night, you will see a lot more drunks sleeping it off in the road."

Barry stayed at the Sandy Lane Hotel. His ground floor room led straight out on to a patio on which, in addition to the usual table and chairs, stood a large refrigerator full of cold drinks and then across a small lawn to the beach. Every morning Barry would swim out to a raft to lay in the sun before having breakfast.

On the second day he attended the usual meeting to discuss sales ideas and other items. One of the other top partners demonstrated his new idea, a graph he would prepare for each client. He introduced it as a new method of showing a client when money could be provided throughout his or her lifetime when needed, such as for school fees, gifts and retirement etc. What amazed Barry was that he had developed an identical graph and had been presenting it to his clients for the last two years!

The following day they all boarded a pirate galleon which set sail around the island. On the main deck were two large wooden barrels, one full of rum and the other of ice from which everyone just helped themselves. There was the usual plank run out on the starboard side and a long rope with a knot on the end. The rope was tied at the top on a spar set up in the rigging. Some were made to walk the plank, others were sent over the side holding on to the rope. Most of them were, of course, drunk at the time!

Barry was not feeling so great, his chest was tight, and he had a slight cough. He asked reception for details of local Doctors, and they phoned to book an appointment for him. "Just take a taxi from out the front and he will take you there," the receptionist said.

Arriving at the surgery, Barry was greeted by a very smart, big black nurse. "Come this way."

They walked into a ward with about eight beds, all bar one had people laying in them. To one side down the length of the ward a low partition divided the room and on the other side sat a number of people waiting to see a Doctor. He was told to sit down, and a Doctor would see him shortly. Everyone was very friendly asking questions: where was he staying? Did he like Barbados? etc. Barry was the only white person – it would seem – in the place.

He was called into the Doctor's room and after a quick examination the Doctor, who turned out to be white, said, "You have bronchitis, from the air conditioning on the plane coming over." The Doctor then spent the next thirty minutes asking questions about the UK.

The next day, Barry was feeling a little better and, having noticed there was one other single chap at the convention, decided to ask if he would like to go on a trip around the island. He agreed and they hired a taxi.

Chatting to the driver, who was pointing out the sights, many of which seemed to have been named after places in the UK, he said, "I will take you up to Aberdeen and show you the sugar cane."

Nearing the top of the hill Barry noticed two big young black fellows standing in a lay-by. Each had a stick of sugar cane and were stripping off the bark with large machetes.

"Pull in," said Barry.

"No, man, they're not nice boys."

"Come on, they won't be any problem."

The driver pulled in but did not get out of the taxi. Barry approached the lads.

"Hello."

"Hi, man, would you like some sugar cane?"

"I'll try some," said Barry as he was joined by his fellow passenger. They both stood there sucking the cane which was very sweet. Barry asked why they were not at work, and they told him there wasn't any available.

As Barry and his friend left, they gave the lads some money and thanked them.

One morning as he was walking along the beach, Barry was approached by a slim, older woman carrying a basket on her head. She opened her mouth to speak. He noticed that she only had two front teeth.

"Do you want some?" she said, mentioning some local drug. "It make you happy."

"No thanks," said Barry.

"We go to your room, I give you good time," she said.

"I'm meeting someone, can't stop," said Barry, looking along the beach as he tried to get away.

# Chapter 36

## Seminars

A letter arrived from the Inland Revenue, Chatham, requesting Barry's attendance at a meeting at their offices. Barry had yet to learn to write back asking them to state, in detail, what they wished to discuss before he agreed to attend. He sent a copy of the letter to his accountant and even he did not tell him to request details before attending.

The tax office was in a small tower block overlooking the River Medway. It was built on concrete pillars with car parking underneath and at the back. Barry, who had arrived by car with his accountant, parked under the tower block. Entering he asked for Mr Smith.

"Please take a seat, he will be down in a moment."

Barry and his accountant sat there, not speaking for what seemed like ages when the lift doors opened and a slim man in his late thirties walked towards them.

"Sorry to keep you waiting," his hand out ready to shake as Barry proffered his hand. "Let's go up to my office."

They entered an office on the fourth floor which overlooked the river. It was quite empty with just a table and four chairs.

"Do sit down," said the young man, pointing to two chairs facing the desk. He then became more serious and pointed to an open tape-recording machine.

"As you can see there is no tape in the machine so our conversation will not be recorded."

Barry felt his temper rising; what was going on? He thought this was more like a Police investigation!

The tax inspector continued, "These so-called seminars you run on the Olau Line, they are just a jolly!" That was it! Barry got up from his chair and started to pace the room. He was in a fury, still pacing, whilst he looked out of the window at the calm river flowing down to the sea. He began to calm down.

Looking across to the inspector, who had gone a little white in the face, Barry said, "You have no idea; sitting in a lecture room for a day, listening to professionals, taking notes and filling in questionnaires, THAT'S A JOLLY?"

The inspector stood up and put out his hand to shake Barry's. "Thank you for coming," and he walked towards the door. Barry and his accountant followed him into the lift.

As they walked under the building to the car park Barry said to his accountant, "As I drive out, look over to the entrance and you will see him standing there looking to see what car I am driving." Barry was right; he was standing looking out at them and the car.

About two months later Barry received a tax refund.

Over the years Barry had learned to cultivate a good relationship with his bankers. He tried to get to know them, their interests and their backgrounds. He understood there had to be mutual trust so that whatever proposal he put forward would have a good chance of success. However, over the years, for one reason or another, there were times when a relationship broke down. In the very early years when Barry was struggling to get the business off the ground, he banked at Barclays at London Bridge. The manager at the time was Stan Carslake. Stan looked like Sid James from the 'Carry On' films. Whenever you met him, he always had a joke to tell, making you relaxed and feeling good. He was a very clever man with a bevy of beautiful young ladies on the tills to attract the traders from Borough Market across the road from the bank.

The bank moved Stan to the Fleet Street branch about a year later and Barry inherited a new manager. Barry was called in to meet him, wondering why as he travelled up from Dartford.

On entering the bank, as Barry sat waiting to meet the manager, he felt the atmosphere in the banking hall seemed to be colder: fewer smiles from the staff, no laughter.

Ushered into the office, Barry was met by a very tall, unsmiling man in a grey suit. "We no longer want your business, please close your account," he said looking down on Barry.

Barry walked out in a daze. He knew his account was not very big or active, having just lost the engineering companies, but what a way to treat a customer!

Barry walked across the road, down Borough High Street and came to a large branch of NatWest Bank. Still smarting, he thought, *Why not?* and went in.

"Is the manager available?" he asked a young lady at the counter.

"What is it about, Sir?"

"I wish to open an account."

"If you would like to take a seat, I'll see if he is available."

Minutes later a slim man, who Barry estimated to be in his early forties, approached and introduced himself. "My name is Tony Pyne," he said holding out his hand.

Thus began a great, friendly business arrangement. Once when Barry was going through a difficult time, he said, "I believe you will make it."

At Rotary there was the usual number of professionals: solicitors, accountants, bankers etc. In those days, two from each were allowed to join. In the Rochester club there were managers from Midland Bank and from Lloyds Bank; the latter went by the name of Andrew Barker. Always looking for new business for the bank and its clients, Andrew began to promote a local business and dining club which his bank helped to finance. He also tried to persuade fellow Rotarians to bank with him.

It seemed strange to Barry when, in the course of promoting his business, he sent a letter inviting Rotarians to a seminar and received a telling off! Yet Andrew got off scot-free promoting his bank!

Sadly, a few years latter Andrew died of a heart attack when attending a service at Canterbury Cathedral. A lady was appointed in his place as Manager of Lloyds Bank, Rochester, and soon afterwards Barry received a phone call to tell him to close his account and repay a small overdraft. As it happened, with two main banking accounts he did not need this small personal account. Strange how some banking officers don't have people skills.

One November day, Barry received an invitation, out of the blue, to a Christmas Party at Coutts Bank, one of the world's oldest banks and bankers to the Queen. Unfortunately, he had to decline as he would be away skiing with his family.

Barry, having been in the finance business for many years, had met a great many nice, pleasant, people, some not only became clients but also close friends. His contact list for referrals included bankers, GPs, accountants and solicitors who would recommend him to their clients, be it to arrange finance, save tax, investment or protection and much more.

His parents decided to sell their house and retire to the coast, and they contacted a local solicitor to deal with the conveyancing.

"Pop, would you mind if I contacted your solicitor?" Barry asked his father.

"What for?"

"To see if he could refer me to any of his clients."

"I don't mind, you go ahead."

Having arranged an appointment over the phone, Barry turned up at the solicitor's offices and parked his car in front of a large (what seemed to be) house. He was shown into a room and the young lady said, "Mr Bishop will not be long."

Mr Bishop came in a few minutes later. He was taller than Barry and he thought about fifteen or more years older. Later, as Barry got to know him, he learned that he was at Nuremburg working at the war trials. Barry had no idea how he managed with his affliction. Reg Bishop had the worse stutter Barry had ever met. As he tried to get the words out, he would bend his head back, open his mouth and close his eyes, facing the ceiling. The more he tried to talk the worse his stutter became.

Reg introduced him to his sister and her husband, who had retired and moved to a bungalow on the coast. When Barry first met Tommy and Vicky Sowden he was pleasantly surprised by the greeting. He was shown into the lounge and offered a seat facing Tommy who sat opposite. Alongside their chairs were small side tables. Behind and slightly to one side of Tommy, so that Barry could see it in full, hung a very large painting. The picture was of a rotund gentleman with large side whiskers, in a red hunting coat, a white waist coat and smoking a briar pipe. The frame was large and very ornate; the picture was not suitable for a modern bungalow. It seemed to Barry that he had been placed in that particular chair to admire the painting.

"Do you like the portrait of my great, great, great grandfather? My family had a large estate in those days, down in the west country."

Barry, Tommy, Vicky and later Mavis became great friends, so much so that as time went by, they asked if Mavis would like to buy some of their collection of crockery. They used to own an upmarket shop in West London. Mavis purchased a hand painted 12-piece tea set.

Turning to financial matters, Tommy, who was nearly 15 years older than Vicky, asked Barry if he could he arrange their income to last till they both died. Unfortunately, Barry did not possess a crystal ball, not that he would be able to read it if he did!

"I'll look at your investments, make some assumptions and prepare some ideas but, as you must know, I cannot predict the future."

A few years later Tommy died in his eighties, and within six months Vicky passed away. Their income did not run out!

Before they died, Tommy and Vicky introduced Barry to two retired teachers, both widows. They lived in North West London and were great friends, and Barry would visit them once a year to check on their investments. They looked forward to his visits and on occasion would take him to lunch.

They developed a signalling system whereby one would tell the other that Barry was leaving and would be with them shortly. Whoever was the first to be visited would phone the other, let the number ring three times and put down the phone. The first lady lived in an apartment, the other in a very nice bungalow with a large back garden. Barry always talked about their families who had children of their own. Over time, Barry, if he had time, would carry out odd jobs such as painting the ceiling or repairing a door for the lady in the bungalow. He would always know in advance and take his old clothes with him. Mrs H. would greet him at the front door with a big hug and a kiss on the cheek. When shown into the back living room there would be an easy chair where Barry would sit. On the side table would be a glass and a bottle of whisky. Mrs H would sit in the chair opposite with all her current paperwork and her glass ready to be filled.

One very hot summer day Barry arrived at the front door in his suit and tie feeling very hot and sweaty. Mrs H greeted him in her usual way. "Let's go through to the garden," she said, "take your jacket off." In the garden there was an open fold up canvas chair and a deck chair. "You sit in the chair, Barry, and I'll sit in the deck chair." She proceeded to lie down, pull up her frock to show her knickers and said, "Let me run you a nice cool bath and I will wash your back!"

With the success of his seminars on the Olau Line, Barry was considering going up-market with the venues to try to attract more wealthy clients. However, circumstances gave him the opportunity quicker than he expected. He received a telephone call from a council officer he knew.

"Barry, the council has hired the Orient Express to promote Rochester and the Medway towns and we have a spare carriage. Would you like to hire it for the day?"

"Where is it going to and where do we board it?"

"Rochester to Folkestone where it stops for around three hours or so. Late afternoon tea will be served on the way back and it terminates at Victoria."

Barry agreed to hire the one carriage and Joan and he set about finding a venue to hold a seminar while the train was at Folkestone. They arranged a meeting room at the Imperial Hotel.

Both Joan and Barry agreed the train was better than they had anticipated. The polished wood, the overall décor was straight out of the 1920s, absolute luxury, and the service was as good, or better, than most five-star hotels.

Alighting back at Victoria Station, Barry, Joan and their secretary were walking together towards the exit when the secretary put her hand in her handbag and took out a small pill box with the Orient Express logo on the lid. "Look what I've nicked," she said, looking quite pleased with herself.

Barry went bonkers. He was really angry. His face screwed up, and as he turned and bent down, he looked her in her face and said in a threatening voice, "If you ever do anything like that again, you're fired!"

During the 1980s and early 1990s there were many overseas conventions: Greece, the Caribbean, Bangkok, Monte Carlo and lots more, many of which Barry and Mavis declined to attend, mostly because Mavis did not like to travel. Each year Barry qualified to receive gifts: up-market office furniture, Stuart Devlin silverware, David Shepherd numbered prints and many more.

The annual London conventions were held in a different venue each year and the top attendees always stayed overnight in five-star hotels. One year the whole of the Albert Hall was taken over for the convention. In the boxes around eight to ten top presidents and their wives were seated. To the rear of the box on the level near the entrance was a table laid with a white table cloth on which were bottles of whisky, gin and other alcoholic beverages. During the motivational performance, lights shone off the stage and picked out each top president as he stood up. It reminded Barry of the Second World War and the search lights! For lunch, each person had a Fortnum & Mason hamper containing, among other goodies, caviar, smoked salmon and Champagne.

# Chapter 37

# The Demon Drink

Six of the Falcon Club members and their wives decided to go out for dinner one evening on the night before the annual convention. They met in the hotel bar, the men taking turns to buy a round of drinks, prior to moving on to a restaurant. On arrival at a nearby establishment, they must have given the manager the impression they were going to be a bit rowdy as he placed them on a table for six at the very back of the restaurant. More drinks were ordered while they waited for the food to be served.

Mavis turned to Barry. As more white wine was poured into Barry's glass, Mavis turned to him and said, in a loud voice, "NO MORE!" as he reached to pick up the wine glass. Being slightly pissed, the alcohol beginning to affect his brain, Barry started to argue. He glanced around and could see that the others were looking at him as though he was under Mavis's thumb and were awaiting his reaction. So, Barry stood up, glass in hand, and threw the wine over Mavis's head. All hell let loose!

Mavis and Barry had no dinner that night and he slept in the other bedroom of the suite in which they were staying.

Barry had always liked a drink – this was not the first time he had taken too much – which led him to change his behaviour.

He had been to see one of his clients who also liked a whisky. They started to get into a session and Barry forgot he had a client meeting in his office later that same afternoon. Mavis would sometimes call into see Joan or him at his office. As it happened, she called in that very day.

Joan would usually leave the office at 3.30pm, however, the client arrived, and Joan and Mavis entertained him with coffee and chat, but still Barry did not show. Joan left late and Mavis stayed talking to the client for another hour, but in the end the client said he had to leave. Some two hours later Barry drove into the gravel car park at the rear of the office, just as Mavis came out to get into her car.

"Where have you been?" she shouted. "You have been drinking!" still shouting as she walked towards his car showing her anger. "You had a client waiting for you."

Anger welling up, Barry got more and more annoyed and spun the car around in a very fast turn, spraying gravel all over Mavis. He was drunk. As he drove up the A2 towards Dartford he started to realise he had to get off the road before he had an accident. He turned off into the Inn on the Lake Hotel car park.

"Hav-zu aa rooms," as he threw his Amex card down on the reception desk.

"Yes, Sir," said the young lady, ignoring the fact that he was pissed.

Taking his room key, Barry made his way down the hallway, bouncing off the walls on his way to the room. He managed to take his shoes and jacket off before collapsing on the bed and snoring with his mouth open.

Some hours later he was woken as someone started to shake him. "Barry, wake up, wake up."

"Leave me alone, I want to sleep." With one eye closed, he glanced up to see Mavis and the receptionist standing by the bedside.

They left him to sleep and next day Mavis came to pick him up.

"How did you find me?"

"Well, I rang round to see if you found a bed with some off our friends. Then I tried a few hotels and as I was driving down the A2 I noticed your car parked. I managed to persuade the receptionist to let me in the room with her pass key."

In addition to being a member of Rotary and the Rochester Pickwick Club, Barry was invited to join the FART club and received the following letter:

*Dear FART*

*Welcome to the ranks of the finest Auslander (foreigners) Racing Team. You are now an official FART and we hope you will live up to the principles of the club: FUN!!*

*FART was first witnessed in the spring of 1976 in Soll in Austria. The Auslanders were celebrating, just a little, in the Post Hotel's Ski Bar following Canadian Peter's triumphant third placing in the Soll ski instructors' race. It is not every day that foreigners reach such heights in Austrian ski schools. The Auslanders had consolidated their position.*

*The traditional FARTing ceremony involves the singing of the FART song and the taking of the schnapps. The FART salute (the left hand over the left eye) was devised so that the schnapps could be held in most people's more stable right hand to avoid spillage. The covering of the eye was in order to overcome the problem of seeing double. The ape stems from the early "Not bad for a Gorilla" skiing position.*

These were printed on various shirts.

Mark Weinberg, Chairman of Allied Dunbar (later to become Sir), was asked by the Government to propose new regulations for the selling of some financial products such as assurance, pensions and investment bonds.

After the recommendations came into force, Barry's means of obtaining introductions and referrals had to change. These regulations had a big effect on income for his business as he could no longer obtain introductions from solicitors, bank managers and others for assurance products. However, he could still assist in obtaining finance and introductions to other lenders. Whereas in the past he could sell products which were not in the Allied Dunbar portfolio, this was not now possible. The amount of bureaucracy increased; more reports, more internal and external exams, more inspections and more record keeping leading to less time to find and meet new clients or service current and old clients.

Barry's tenants, who occupied the top two floors of his office building, mentioned to Joan that they may have to hand back their lease early. The National Dock Labour Board was being disbanded, which would mean a further loss of income. Some weeks later the tenants moved out and Barry received a phone call from an accountant acting for the Government regarding the remaining time left on the lease. After introductions he said, "We propose to hand back the lease."

"You can't just hand it back, you have to pay the remaining rent."

"But you can easily re-let."

"No, we can't, anyway you will still have to pay the remaining rent."

Eventually they came to a compromise and a cheque was received.

Around about the same time, the tenants on the ground and basement floors also left, leaving these areas empty and no rent coming in.

Over the next two years, times were hard for both the garden centres and Barry's sole remaining tenant. His tenant in the property on the other side of the High Street, where he was trading as a restaurant, asked if he could hand back his lease which had one year left to run.

Barry decided it was pointless to demand a year's rent as the tenant did not have the money. With the commercial market as it was, he decided to sell the property. Of his small property portfolio, he only had his office, which was unencumbered, and the apartment with a small mortgage. This was let out under a shorthold tenancy.

The garden centre, which was a joint freehold with his partner, was mortgaged to Midland Bank. This included the redevelopment loan for the new buildings. The local Midland Bank Manager phoned Barry one day and asked if he could help a lady who was trying to raise funds for a business venture.

"Barry, this lady was in business with her sister, and they have broken up the partnership. Do you think you can help?"

"Give her my number and ask her to phone me and I'll see what I can do."

On the day of her appointment, Joan showed the lady into Barry's office. The grey-haired lady, who appeared to be in her early sixties, sat on the leather chesterfield and Barry sat in the matching chair to one side which was slightly higher. This was the method he used when interviewing prospective clients.

"Tell me about the business you and your sister ran."

"My sister and I set up the business some years ago. We supplied attractive ladies to department stores and various companies to promote their products."

"Where did you find these ladies?"

"We advertised and asked them to send in a photo with details of any past experience. I have a portfolio with me; it gives details of the ladies that were on our books. When you go into large stores, you will see some of our ladies on the makeup and perfume counters."

Barry looked through the folder which contained hundreds of photographs of very attractive ladies. He continued to carry out the fact-find, but discovered that she had not prepared a business plan or a cash flow forecast.

A few weeks later Barry asked her to come and see him at the office where he presented his proposals which included life cover on herself and her husband to protect each other in the event of death by repaying any loans. She said that she did not want her husband covered nor would he.

There followed a long period of trying to convince her. Joan came into the office and explained the details, both of them going through the problems she would face if either of them died. However, the lady refused to ask her husband to come in to see Barry or take any cover on his life.

Barry arranged the start-up finance. Little did he know then that the lady was going to present him with a problem in the future!

# Chapter 38

# Czechoslovakia

Mavis was not keen on flying and was quite happy for Barry to drive to Austria. They would travel through parts of France, Belgium and Germany to their apartment in Soll, Austria, which was just off the Inn Valley. It would normally take 10 hours by car. From the apartment, which acted like a hub at the centre of a wheel, they would drive to nearby countries. It had one bedroom, a lounge with a convertible settee which could be made into a double bed and a mezzanine floor with a single bed set over the small kitchen. Off of this were a shower room and toilet. Sometimes they would take friends with them, mostly in the summer, and travel to other countries where they would stay for a few days.

On one occasion Cyril and Rosalie joined them and they decided to go to Prague in Czechoslovakia. The country had gained its freedom from Russia and border crossings had started to open and Westerners could enter. Barry decided to enter at the nearest crossing north of Linz.

Some of the Russians were still there but the Czechs had gained their independence. The four of them planned to look for a small hotel near the border, cross over north of Linz and spend the next day in Prague.

The area north of Linz was flat, not like the Tyrol. Barry drove to the border. On reaching the crossing, he turned the car around and drove back to the nearest village, topping up the fuel at a small local garage where a man served them.

"Bitte, hav'ez hotel – zimmer?" said Barry attempting to speak German.

"Ya, links," said the attendant pointing back towards the border and indicating left.

Following the instructions, they found themselves on a small country road which reminded them of the roads and fields of France. As they entered a village, which had no pavements, the sides of the roads became dusty with dark yellow sand. Small, mature trees had been planted at intervals at the side of what seemed to be the only main street. The sand went up to the buildings. The village was empty, or so it seemed, as there was no one about. Barry pulled into the side and stopped the car as Cyril said, "Is that a hotel over there?" pointing at a dusty stone building.

"It looks a bit rough," said Mavis. "Let's go and have a look."

Barry and Cyril crossed the road to the hotel entrance which was set back in the wall. Walking up the steps they were faced with massive, ornately carved, wooden double doors. Pushing one side, the door silently swung open.

They looked around in utter surprise, the entrance hall was large, the floor was marble and shone in the light and the wood reception desk cast its shadow over the floor.

"Guten abend," said a lovely lady in a long white coat.

"Good evening, hav'nz zwei double zimmer mit douche," said, Barry still trying to speak German!

"Ya, comonz," said the lady, turning to walk down a passage and then up a short flight of stairs.

The rooms were luxurious, the beds comfortable and Mavis and Rosalie were surprised and very pleased. That evening they had very nice dinner with wine and other drinks. Slightly merry, they were laughing most of the evening and slept soundly that night. Next morning having paid the bill, which was surprisingly inexpensive, the whole of the staff lined up to shake everyone's hands as they said goodbye.

On reaching the border, they stopped the car and got out to join the short queue. Standing awaiting their turn in the small building, Barry noticed a sign in English and

German informing them they had to have some sort of document, before they could enter Czechoslovakia. It also read that this could be obtained from a machine on the Austrian side of the border. Barry and Cyril ran back to find the machine whilst Mavis and Rosalie held their place in the line. Having paid for the documents, Barry and Cyril returned, out of breath, and took up their places again. They were nearing the front, only two more to go, when a man pushed to the front of the queue and going down on his knees said, in English, to the lady behind the glass panel, "Excuse me, where do I buy the petrol coupons?"

"You can only purchase them at a Bank in Prague."

*Petrol coupons*, thought Barry, "I have a Land Rover! There's no way we are going to get back to Austria from Prague on the one full tank. I'll have to buy some coupons in Prague."

As they drove towards the city, they noticed every village had a loud speaker fixed to one of the poles that held various cables. Entering the city Barry could not find any car parks so he parked on a main street. Looking around they came across an upturned Russian tank lying on its side with a Czech soldier in full gear, including his rifle, standing alongside. The tank had a flower sticking out of its gun. The underside, or bottom, of the tank had graffiti sprayed on it, one being 'Russians Fuck Off!' in English. When they got back to Austria, Barry picked up a day-old copy of The Times newspaper and there on the front page was a photograph of the same tank.

Feeling hungry, they started to look for a restaurant, eventually finding one in a basement under a large building. On entering, they found themselves in a long queue of people. They stood in line for a short while and all that Barry could think of was 'Petrol coupons'!

Barry decided to take the initiative and moved into the restaurant and in a loud voice, almost shouting, he said, "Can anyone speak English?"

Almost immediately an old man approached him. "I speak a little English."

Holding out his hand, as though to shake the old man's hand, Barry held a note of very small value and said, "We are in a hurry and must get to a meeting, can you find us a table?"

"Come this way, Sir," and moved to a corner table set in an alcove.

As they all sat down, Barry said, "Order me something to eat. I have to find a Bank to purchase fuel coupons."

Walking down the street, Barry looked up at the buildings hoping to see the word 'Bank'. Having found one he approached the entrance only to find a locked iron gate. He began to wonder if all the banks were closed. Walking on, he at last found a bank that was open. Entering through two massive doors he was surprised to find himself in a very great room with a high ceiling at least four floors high. The walls and supporting columns were all stone. At the far wall there was a massive stone staircase set between statues, just like a Royal Palace. Looking around there were no desks or banking counters, so Barry started to walk up the stairs. As he got further up, he could hear people talking. At the top the room opened up with four or five banking positions all of which had long queues waiting to be seen; the signs above each were all in Czech.

*Where the hell do I get these coupons from... which queue?* thought Barry. He then had a stroke of luck when he heard English being spoken by someone in the middle of a queue.

"Excuse me; do you know which queue it is for the petrol coupons?"

"Yes, it's this one."

Thanking him, Barry joined the end of the queue. After about twenty minutes he arrived at the counter.

"Can I have some petrol coupons?" said Barry addressing the woman who was sitting high up behind the screen.

"Which currency?" came the answer in broken English. "You only pay in Western currency."

As luck would have it, having travelled across Europe, Barry had French and Swiss francs, German marks, Austrian schillings and English pounds.

He paid with Swiss francs and waited to collect the coupons. The lady gave him a ticket which he assumed was the receipt for the money.

"Where are the coupons?"

"You go next queue."

With a big sigh, Barry joined the next queue thinking about the others tucking into their food, and possibly wondering where he had got to.

Having at last met up, Barry with the coupons in his pocket, the four of them had another short walk around the city before they made their way back to the apartment.

Sometime later Barry spotted what looked like a petrol station. It only had one dim light shining on a pump and he pulled in. It was early evening and getting darker and the ladies had an urgent need for the use of a loo. As Barry got out of the car a man approached out of the darkness with a leather bag hanging over his shoulder, just like a bus conductor's bag. As the man started to fill the fuel tank, Barry said, "Toilet, WC?" He pointed to the end of the building. Cyril and Barry watched the girls almost running to the toilet. "Too much Sec," said one.

As they waited, they could hear the giggling coming from the loo.

"What was all that about?" Barry asked on their return.

"There's a lady sitting at a desk just outside the entrance with her hand out. We both gave her some money and she gave each of us one little square of toilet paper, and you know how big Rosalie is!" she said. 'What am I to do with this?' We just fell about laughing."

# Chapter 39

# Fifty

Times were becoming increasingly difficult. The garden centre was not showing a profit and being reliant on the weather, with two bad springs in a row, made it very difficult for the business to survive. Barry was also finding it more difficult, under the new rules, to obtain introductions for new business.

Having spent some time looking at alternatives, Barry made a personal decision and presented his plan to his partner and wife in the garden centre. They all agreed to sell the site for a housing development.

Having found two interested developers, Barry contacted Midland Bank, who had loaned the money for the centre's redevelopment, and his solicitor. Barry's partner and wife were living on the site in a bungalow which was mortgaged, and which would have to be repaid, so they had to find somewhere else to live. They would continue to run the other garden centre with the stock left after the sale of the current centre transferred to them.

Barry, having put on his negotiating hat – so to speak – pitched the two interested parties against each other and after a month or two one dropped out. The day after the sale was completed and monies transferred, Barry had a telephone call from the Midland Bank Manager who sighed with relief as he thanked Barry. He must have thought that the loan was going to turn into a bad debt and be set against his name at the Bank!

The big weekend was approaching, and Mavis kept on saying to Barry, "Where are we going?" It was Mavis's

50$^{th}$ birthday and Barry, with Joan's help, had organised a weekend away with a few friends.

Barry replied, "You will see."

The two of them set off by car joining the M25 westbound. Sometime later Mavis said, "I know, we are going to Brighton."

"Wait and see!"

For a while it went quiet until Barry drove past the exit on to the M23 to Brighton. "We are going to that hotel where we stayed for one night on the way to our honeymoon!" As they travelled further west Mavis kept trying to guess where they were going. After some time, she gave up.

Arriving at the hotel in Cheltenham, Mavis admitted she would never have guessed this town for their weekend away. Checking in at reception, Barry was pleased that no one had mentioned the word 'party'. Mavis knew that Elizabeth would be attending so she was not surprised when Barry answered the door to their room and Elizabeth walked in. Mavis was sitting in front of the dressing table, preparing her hair ready for dinner. Whilst the two of them were chatting, Barry said, "I won't be a moment, just going to check on our table."

The hotel had two private rooms either side of a hallway leading to the bar and the front reception. Barry had arranged for one room to host a champagne function for Mavis and her guests (who she did not know were coming). The other room was being set up for a private dinner party for sixteen, including the hosts. The time came for Mavis to meet her guests and she assumed that the three of them would be going to have some drinks in the bar before dining. Walking down the hallway they could hear talking coming from a room on their right. "Sounds like someone's having a party in there," said Mavis.

Barry put his hand on the door handle and as he slowly opened the door, he said, "I'm going to have a quick look."

Mavis grabbed Barry's arm and said, "You can't do that!" Just at that moment the door flew open, and someone started the singing off with 'Happy Birthday'.

Dinner was going well as they were all becoming quite merry. They were telling stories between courses when Mavis turned to Barry, who was sitting next to her, "Someone is missing; that place next to you is laid up and no one is sitting there." At that moment there was a tap on the door and in walked Matt Seymour, one of Elizabeth's old boyfriends. He soon joined in the fun as the food and drink flowed. At the end of the meal Barry, alias Wardle, explained some of the toasts used by the Pickwick Club and the fines imposed if seen to be drinking alone.

Mavis started to giggle as she pointed to Matt, "You've got odd socks on." Matt looked down in his semi-drunken state and started to laugh. With all her friends well-oiled that started the laughter off. It got worse – or better if you were drunk – as they all tried to stand, turn to the person sitting next to them, who also had to stand, and say, "I drink to thee, friend, as you drink to your friend, I drink to thee. The more we drink together friends the merrier we shall be. Cheers!" That, of course, is the sober version.

The next evening Barry had arranged for a coach to pick them all up and take them to the theatre for dinner and a show. The coach arrived and Barry went out to see the driver. Unfortunately, everyone started to follow him in order to board the coach. 'Unfortunate' because, to say the least, the coach was in a bad state. It was dirty, some of the so-called leather seats were torn, and the driver was not much better. He was fat, unshaven and scruffy. However, everyone found it funny as they started chatting away. The coach arrived on the opposite side of the road to the theatre, and they all began to point and laugh as someone said, "Look at the nude ladies who have come to greet us!"

There in a shop window were eight or ten naked costume dummies.

# Chapter 40

# Club, Seminar and Wedding

Barry enjoyed his membership of The Rochester Pickwick Club and prepared a short version of some of the rules, a copy of which he always carried with him. People would ask about the club, what they did, the characters' names, etc. He would show them the card and proceed to tell them about some of their activities.

*The Rochester Pickwick Club*
*Founded: Monday the 3rd day of September 1984*

***The Aims & Objects of 'The Club'***
*To perpetuate the name and memory of Charles John Huffam Dickens (1812–1870)*

***Membership***
*Full Membership, which shall be limited to 12 in number, is by invitation only.*

***Duties and Responsibilities***
*On admission to membership the member will be allocated a character title from 'The Posthumous Papers of the Pickwick Club'. The member will beholden to dress and act, as far as is reasonably possible, to mirror that character's description.*

The club appeared many times on TV, not only in the UK but also in New York and other parts of the USA and in Japan. Some years ago, South East TV wished to film the club at one of its dinners in the Leather Bottle, Cobham (one of the inns Charles Dickens frequented). It took place in summer, and it was very hot! What made it even hotter was that during dinner the windows had to be kept closed and the curtains drawn to keep out noise and light. The lights for the cameras generated even more heat. Every minute or two filming would stop while a lady came around and wiped faces and applied more powder. The sound was picked up from microphones hidden in red napkins and displayed in ceramic flower pots set out around the table.

At such dinners, which all attending were in their character costumes, there were a number of rules and rituals such as:

- All members must only be addressed by their character name. Members who fail to do so were fined a bottle of port!
- Members seen drinking without saying "CHEERS" to others present, were also fined a bottle of port.
- Port had to be passed around the table in the correct manner.
- There was always a reading from 'Pickwick Papers'.
- The Loyal Toast was sung (Old English Toast – 1670), one line of which goes, 'nor yet a rope to hang himself' referring to an enemy of the Queen.

On occasion Cedric Dickens would attend the dinners. He lived in Somerset in a cottage called 'Dingley Dell'.

Some of the other activities included riding on an open top horse-drawn bus up the Strand in London and dining in the open at Covent Garden. While dining, Japanese tourists would keep popping up between the members to take photographs.

Some members represented the City of Rochester (as it then was) at the World Travel Show. They chatted to visitors on the city's stand with three of them visiting the displays of other countries. The Greek stand was divided up so that a number of islands each had a space. Seeing the members in costume, they were invited on to the displays to taste their Metaxa (Greek brandy) whilst telling them about their islands. By the time the members had visited four islands they were very merry!

The club entertained one of the American Pickwick Clubs at dinner in a marquee set in the Rochester Castle moat. Pickwick and Wardle signed copies of Pickwick Papers. Barry explained that his character was formerly Mr Wardle of Dingley Dell (some may have seen his cricket team on the back of the old ten-pound note).

And lots, lots more.

## Chapter 41

## QE2 Seminar

Barry was forever trying to obtain more wealthy clients by attracting them to attend his seminars. He decided to look into holding a seminar on the QE2 and a representative from Cunard came to his office to discuss the arrangements and prices. After checking with Barry, Joan and the Cunard representative settled on a cruise to Lisbon in Portugal. It was agreed that he could use the Captain's board room for the seminar meeting. Arrangements were also made for flowers and a half bottle of champagne to be placed in the cabin of each of Barry's guests. For the more expensive seminars Barry would charge the attendees, at a discount, and he would pay the balance.

All went well on the way out: the sea was flat, the seminar went well and in the evening after dinner and entertainment many danced the night away. After the ship docked there was a full day in Lisbon. Having had an enjoyable day, they were looking forward to the entertainment on the way back. What they did not know was that the weather was about to take a turn for the worse. They were going to sail through a hurricane!

Once at sea, the Captain made an announcement: "Ladies and Gentlemen, we are about to sail into some rough weather. Please take advantage of the medical facilities on board if you are feeling unwell."

By early evening the decks and passageways were empty of passengers except for the area outside the Doctor's surgery. Mavis and Joan felt so ill that they were confined to their beds. Mavis stuck to her sea sickness tablets with the Doctor calling on Joan to give her an injection.

Barry went up to the Britannia Restaurant for dinner. The place was almost empty and only four of his party had turned up for dinner. The restaurant would normally have a few hundred people dining.

The modus operandi used at seminars was for prospective clients to fill in a questionnaire and these were collected at the end of question time. Whatever they wrote in answer to the questions gave Barry a reason to contact them in the future. If he did not acquire any new clients, he was out of pocket. The QE2 trip cost him a lot of money!

It was some months later when Barry was telling an associate who used to be in the industry about the loss he had incurred from his QE2 Seminar; he told Barry about a friend of his who would travel on the QE2 every year. This friend, who was an associate with Abbey Life, would purchase a nearly new Rolls Royce, use it for some months and then ship it to the USA on the QE2. Travelling on the same passage, he would obtain UK clients from the passengers by arranging meetings for when they returned to the UK. On arrival in New York, he would sell the Rolls at a very considerable profit, have a holiday and earn commission from new, very wealthy clients.

# Chapter 42

# The Wedding

Barry would sometimes do crazy things and this day was no exception. He pulled into a service station to fill up with fuel and in front of him a mother was filling up her car with just £10 of petrol. In the back seat there were two children playing. The car was a little run down and the kids, judging by their clothes, gave the impression that the family did not have a lot of money. Christmas was approaching, and as Barry went to pay for his fuel, the mother of the children was just about to pay for her fuel. "Just a moment," Barry said. "I'll pay for this lady's fuel as well." He turned to the mother and said, "There is only one condition, you use your ten pounds to buy something for the kids."

It was early spring of 1991 and Mavis and Barry's only daughter, Elizabeth, was hoping to get married in October 1993. She had set her heart on getting married in Rochester Cathedral but both mother and daughter were having trouble making a booking. They were being given the run around by the person in charge. In fact, at one point he refused to give permission.

After having spent another two weeks trying to get permission and a date, they tearfully asked Barry if he could try and help.

Barry set about doing some research. First, he spoke to people he knew who regularly attended services to ask for the name of the person to contact. Try as he might, he could not get through to him. After some days of asking people, he had a breakthrough. He was told that the person he needed to speak to sometimes called into a local pub at lunchtime.

Barry and a friend who worked in his office, also named Barry, decided to pop into the pub at lunchtime in the hope of meeting the chap. On their second visit the person came in to the back bar and ordered a pint. The two Barrys were sitting at the back of the bar and Barry (the father of the intended bride) got up and approached the cathedral's representative. "Can I buy you a drink? What would you like?"

The chap turned to face Barry and said, "You must be the chap who keeps phoning to try and book your daughter's wedding date?"

"That's right."

"Let's finish our drinks and go over to my house and I'll get the diary out."

His house was a two up, two down, set in a terrace of around six houses belonging to the cathedral. The ladies were over the moon when Barry told them he had booked the wedding for 3rd October 1992.

The big day came. The massive doors to the cathedral opened as the families and guests filed in. The ringing of the cathedral bells brought locals and tourists alike to view the bride. Waiting in a side road, an open-top double decker bus was ready to take the guests to the reception in Chatham Dockyard. Visitors to the castle looked down from the battlements to view the proceedings. Then it started, just a fine light rain as Barry and his daughter entered to sound of the cathedral's massive organ.

In the dockyard was a large house with a garden, known as the Commissioner's House, which had become a private members club. A marquee was set in the garden where the reception was being held. The bridegroom, Matt, had appointed one of his friends, a short chap, as his best man and Mr Pickwick, in full toastmasters outfit complete with bag, officiated.

It was time for the best man's speech. From under the top table Mr Pickwick pulled out a wooden orange box and proceeded to lift up the best man who was slightly the worst for wear and nearly fell off. The assembled company, by now suitably happy from the drink, fell about laughing.

More people joined the evening reception and later Barry announced that the bride and groom were about to leave and would everyone please follow him. The evening entertainment was not yet finished, as they were about to find out as they crossed the road.

Jazz music could be heard coming from the river and looking towards the sound lights could be seen coming from a boat moored alongside the harbour wall. The jazz band was playing on the deck of the Kingswear Castle paddle steamer. Led by Barry and the bride and groom, all the guests boarded for a musical cruise.

# Chapter 43

# New Trade

Times were changing. Barry had been a partner for twenty years with Allied Dunbar, as it was now called. Since he came out of the Army at the age of twenty-three, when he had bet a friend he would be worth a million before him, he had set up two engineering companies employing forty people, sold encyclopaedia whilst employing two machinists, lost both companies and started a ladies hairdressers and children's wear shop and employed two men as jobbing builders at the same time as running the shop. While with Allied Dunbar, Barry had set up a consultancy offering management advice, financial products and introductions to banks and other lenders. He had also invested in two garden centres and built up a small property portfolio; most of the properties now having been sold due to the loss of tenants, reduction in income and a very bad investment.

Allied Dunbar had been sold again and Barry, having known some of the founders of Allied Dunbar, was not surprised when they left to set another company with the help of Lord Jacob Rothschild. Sir Mark Weinberg and Mike Wilson were building a team for the new company, St James's Place Wealth Management, to provide advice and investments for more wealthy clients.

Barry needed another challenge. He contacted one of the new company's managers, whom he happened to know, and asked if he could join them. He told them that he had borrowed £500,000 from his practice value at Allied Dunbar and after a brief interview, the new company said they would pay off the loan and Barry accepted.

Joan and Barry were now rattling around in their respective offices on one floor of Barry's three-storey office building when he received a phone call from Allied Dunbar's Maidstone office.

"Hi, Barry, is there any chance I could temporarily work out of your office. I will be leaving AD soon and joining St James's."

"I would think so, come over and have a chat."

A week later Sid Smith Green met with Joan and Barry, both of whom he knew from their visits to the Maidstone office. Barry decided to let him use the ground floor office. Barry made two mistakes: he did not charge him a rent or get him to sign a lease.

Some weeks later Sid came into Barry's personal office overlooking the Cathedral and introduced an American called Harry.

"I've brought Harry along to see you to tell you about a note trading scheme he is trying to set up. He and I have been looking into the idea of raising funds to set one up but because of the amount of money needed to start trading we need a very rich person or a consortium or a large firm with funds."

Harry started to explain that banks had ratings as did countries which gave other countries and banks an indication of their credit worthiness in a similar way to personal credit ratings. Countries' central banks issue notes which high rated banks then purchase. They then sell them on to lesser rated banks and make a profit. But, of course, the trading did not stop there. The lower rated bank then sells it on to an even lower rated bank and makes a profit. The trading on a particular note only stops when a bank wishes to hold until maturity when the central bank pays out. Trading takes place daily. Harry then went on to explain that the returns or profit on each transaction were measured in fractions of a percent. But as the notes were traded every day, and possibly more than once a day, there would be very large profits.

"What's the minimum amount you need to trade?" asked Barry.

"One million pounds."

When they had left Joan and Barry discussed the scheme. Joan was against the idea and not happy that Harry would be working downstairs.

Discussions continued and Sid and the American spent days working in the ground floor office telephoning possible contacts to try and get them to invest in the scheme. They asked Barry if he would invest and he put in quite a few thousand, unbeknown to Joan who was on holiday at the time.

Diverting from his normal business, Barry contacted one of his corporate bank managers at the Arab Banking Corporation to set up a meeting. Some weeks later he arrived with Sid and Harry at the bank's Moorgate office. Having been shown into the manager's office, they had a short discussion briefly outlining the scheme. The manager said that they would shortly meet with two of the most senior officers in the bank's boardroom. The manager took them in the lift to the next floor and as they came out of the lift they almost stopped in amazement! They were in a very large room bathed in light with a cloistered walkway around the four walls. In the centre a fountain, more like a small waterfall, was flowing into a small pond. Hanging on the back wall was a magnificent painting of an Arab in his white robes, sitting on a white stallion.

The meeting did not go well, as the bank was not interested. Sometime afterwards, when Barry thought about how the meeting had gone, he felt that Harry did not present himself well, even down to his shoes which were scruffy and in need of repair.

Via a friend, Barry made another contact and arranged to meet at the Institute of Directors in Pall Mall. At the meeting, which Barry attended alone, the chap said that he had been able to "get in" on a trade in New Zealand notes and was getting one sixteenth on each trade. He also said that if Barry could raise a million, he would be prepared to help.

Joan returned from her holiday and walked into Barry's office and asked for the bank statements. Joan prepared all the accounts.

"I'll get them in a minute," Barry said as he was concentrating on some documents. This went on for some days with Barry not giving her the statements. He was running around trying to hide them having invested all the money, but he had to give in sometime and face the music. Within an hour of her checking them, Joan flew into his office and verbally let rip! He was in trouble, very bad trouble. If Joan left it would be almost like cutting off his right arm. It took many weeks for it all to calm down.

By now Harry and Sid were no longer working from Barry's office. One day he received a phone call from Sid saying they had managed to raise the money from a large public quoted UK construction company, and they wanted to come and see Barry to give him the full details. During the meeting they mentioned that a meeting to invest the money had been set up in New York and they proposed to go with two of the officers from the company and could Barry help out with their travel costs.

A week or two later Joan buzzed through, "I have Sid on the line from New York. It's all fallen through, and the officers have flown back with the cheque in their pocket."

That was it. Barry was out having lost a packet!

For over two years a court case had been looming. Other than the occasional phone call or letter from his solicitor (appointed by his professional indemnity insurers) requesting more information, nothing seemed to be happening. Some years back Barry had arranged funds for a lady to set up an agency to provide demonstrators and saleswomen on temporary contracts to major stores. She had visited Barry's office on three occasions, and he had prepared a report in which he had insisted that both she and her husband take out life cover to repay the loan, which was to be in both their names, should the company default. However much he tried, she refused to have her husband insured.

Some years later her husband died and shortly after the business failed. The bank then looked to her for the repayment of the loan. Through her solicitors, she then tried to make a claim for bad advice from Barry. He started to receive phone calls from the solicitor acting for him. "It's going to court. It has been withdrawn. She has applied again for legal aid."

This went on for another year until the case was dropped.

# Chapter 44

# Architects

Joan rang through to Barry's office: "Mr Jones on the phone."

"Put him through. Hello, Bob, what can I do for you?"

"Can you find us another bank?"

"What, another one! What have you done to upset the one I introduced you to two years ago?"

Bob went on to explain their architectural practice had got into financial difficulty and they owed money for office rent, their own and staff tax and other creditors.

"Bloody hell! What have you two been up to? I'm not going to be able to find a bank to help you. The only thing I can suggest is for me to come and see you both and go through everything. I will then write a short report and make a recommendation for you to consider. But that will cost you two hundred and fifty pounds."

"We agree, can you come and see us as soon as possible?"

A few days later Barry had a meeting with the two partners before he looked through all the accounts and creditors. During the discussion they informed him that bankruptcy notices had been issued on both them and the partnership. What surprised Barry even more was that they had paid an Insolvency Practitioner from the North of England £20,000 who told them he could save them from becoming bankrupt. It was obvious that the business was in a complete mess and unless something was done within a few weeks, not only would they suffer but the nine employees would have to go.

Having completed his report within a week, Barry presented it to the partners after he had explained, in full, the implications.

Jack said, "Would you mind if my father-in-law had a look at this? He is on his way from Spain where he has retired. He was an architect."

"Not at all, but I would suggest I present the report in case he would like to ask any questions."

Three days later Barry attended the meeting with the two partners and the father-in-law in the partnership offices. They all accepted Barry's proposals.

Having little time to implement, Barry set about forming a limited liability company with a similar name to the partnership. He would own the whole of the share capital. All the staff, including the bankrupt partners, would now be employees of the company. New offices had to be found which Bob set about. Barry would have to guarantee the lease as the company was new. In the meantime, the staff carried on completing the partnership contracts. New quotations and contracts were to be in the limited company's name.

Barry contacted NatWest, his main bankers, and arranged a sizeable loan in order to run the company.

One day, prior to their move to the new offices, a scruffy looking man turned up at reception and Barry was called to deal with him.

"Can I help you?" he said to a short, fat man who stank of cigarette smoke. He had an open neck shirt, buttons undone showing his hairy chest.

"I'm from the Inland Revenue. I'm here to collect tax you owe."

"What's the name of the business?" said Barry.

"Charles Jones."

"That's not us; they went bankrupt."

The man left and Barry turned to the receptionist and commented that the Inland Revenue must be recruiting from the gutter!

Bob came to see Barry a week later holding a form in his hand. "Please sign this."

"What is it?"

"It's the contract for the printer, the machine that prints the plans."

"No, I'm not signing that."

"But you must. We won't be able to work without the machine."

"Leave it with me, I'll sort it."

Barry read through the contract. It was the original one which was signed for by the partnership and related to the machine which was still in use in the office. There was just under £3,000 still to pay over a period of some months which the new company would have to pay. Barry phoned the supplier and giving his name and company said, "We have one of your machines here on our premises, please come and remove it. If it is not removed within seven days, we will be charging you rent."

"But don't you want it?"

"No, but if it's any help, I'll give you a hundred pounds for it."

"Just a minute." Barry could hear the lady talking to someone but could not make out what was said.

"OK, a hundred pounds it is."

That was a saving of over £2,700!

The company was expanding and taking up more and more of his time and inevitably his partnership in St James's was suffering. He had been with them for five years and had still to pay back the remainder of the "transfer fee". Having come to an agreement on a monthly repayment schedule, Barry resigned from St James's.

The architectural company had been trading for over three years. Turnover was six times higher than the last year of the partnership and staff had increased to almost twenty. Then it happened, one of the clients went bust! For some time, they had been discounting their invoices to aid cash flow and the effect on the company could have meant insolvency. Barry had to move quickly. He set up a meeting with the discounters to arrange support. A staff meeting was called where it was agreed that they would only have half salary for one month. Four of them, Joan, Jack, Bob and Barry, would try and collect in as much money as possible from the clients. Barry and Joan would delay paying creditors and the Inland Revenue. It took over four months before the company started to get back on an even keel.

The last bill to be paid was the PAYE. Barry phoned the Inland Revenue to try to come to an arrangement to pay the outstanding debt over a period of time. He spoke to a lady who was very unhelpful and no matter how he tried she refused to give the company time to pay. She must have dealt with the partnership when they defaulted on their repayments!

It was no use, she issued a County Court Judgment (CCJ). Barry had an idea. He knew that if the judgment was published in the papers the company would have many problems with their suppliers, bankers and clients. He turned up at the court and checked in at the Clerk's desk.

"Which party do you act for, plaintiff or defence?" she said looking up at him. He was wearing a suit and tie and had his Rotary pin in the lapel.

"Neither, I'm the defendant."

"Take a seat," she said, looking somewhat surprised.

Barry sat against the far wall from which he could see the whole room and anyone entering. Looking around, he could see that most of them were wearing working clothes, and big dusty boots as if they had just come off a building site. A tall chap came in and walked up to the desk. Barry heard him say, "Anyone here from Charles Jones?"

"Yes, the gentleman sitting over there," she said pointing towards Barry.

The chap, who seemed a bit surprised, turned and walk towards Barry. "Hello, I'm from the Inland Revenue. Shall we go into one of these side rooms and have a chat?" he said pointing to two small rooms only big enough to hold a very small table and two chairs.

Barry had taken with him a large file which had a number of "Post It" notes sticking out for him to find documents.

"I'm here to collect over twenty-eight thousand pounds in overdue tax and National Insurance," he said looking down at his notes.

"I make it a different amount which I have made an offer to pay over three months."

"Why have they not accepted the offer?"

"I don't know, I tried to talk to your colleague and explained that a client had gone bust owing us a lot of money, but she was not helpful."

"We will be going in to see the Judge in his office in a moment."

A lady called out the name of Barry's company and they were shown into the Judge's office. The Judge, dressed in a suit, was sitting at a desk in front of which were two chairs. There were two legal books and a number of files on his desk. Barry, carrying his file with the "Post It" notes, and the Tax Officer, who seemed to only have one piece of paper, were told to sit down. When asked by the Judge, the Tax Officer set out what the Inland Revenue claimed to be owed. Barry set out the amount he said the company owed and then requested a Devlin (*a precedent set by Lord Justice Devlin*).

"I have not come across one of those in years," said the Judge looking somewhat surprised. "Go back outside and agree between you the amount owed. When you have, tell my clerk and she will arrange for you to come back in."

Barry and the Tax Officer went into one of the empty side rooms to agree on the amount for the CCJ. The officer seemed deep in thought and Barry assumed that he did not know what a Devlin was and was waiting on the Judge's decision. Having agreed, they informed the Clerk and sat and waited to be called in to see the Judge. They only had to wait about ten minutes.

"I grant the application for a Devlin. Although this debt will not be published, which I understand will in a small way help your company, the monthly amounts you two have agreed must be paid on time," the Judge said as he looked down at an open book.

Two years later Barry's daughter Elizabeth joined the company. Being a Chartered Surveyor and past Director with Jones Lang Lasalle, she was well suited to help improve the systems to increase profitability. She had left a better paid position in London in order to spend more time with her very young family. After having spent some years with Charles Jones, she was then head hunted by Kent County Council.

The two principal partners in the old partnership were now out of bankruptcy having completed the five years. Barry transferred a share in the company to each of them and retained the balance. The business was growing and becoming more profitable but still paying off loans to NatWest which Barry had personally guaranteed.

One year after transferring the shares, Barry received an offer to buy the business which he reported to Bob and Jack. "What about us?" they said.

"We haven't got that far yet, they have asked for more information. Don't worry, I will keep you informed."

The negotiations went on for some weeks and Barry kept them informed. It must have worried them as they kept coming up with more and more questions and Barry noticed they were holding more meetings than normal with members of staff. One day Bob asked to see Barry in the boardroom.

"Would you accept an offer to purchase the firm from the staff?"

"If it's a fair offer, I would prefer the staff to own the company. But don't forget the Bank loans would have to be repaid before I would sell my shares."

Barry had been thinking of retiring as he had another project in mind. He rejected four offers and agreed to accept the final one once all the loans had been repaid.

Two months later he left.

# Epilogue

Single-minded persons born on the fourteenth have the ability to organise and are happier running their own lives. They like running their own business and are highly motivated. However, they can become bored quickly. Their talent lies in business, sales and advertising, but in relationships they must not be tied down too much.

Milton Keynes UK
Ingram Content Group UK Ltd.
UKHW051054240724
445861UK00016B/332

9 781835 633298